Kathmandu
& the Kingdom of Nepal

Kathmandu and the Kingdom of Nepal
5th edition

Published by
Lonely Planet Publications
PO Box 88, South Yarra 3141, Australia
PO Box 2001A, Berkeley CA 94702 USA

Printed by
Colorcraft, Hong Kong

First Published
1976

This Edition
November, 1985

Photographs
Tony Wheeler

National Library of Australia
Cataloguing in Publication Data

Raj, Prakash A., 1943- Kathmandu and the Kingdom of Nepal

5th ed.
Includes index.
ISBN 0 908086 85 7

1. Nepal – Description and travel – Guide-books.

915.49'604

Prakash A Raj was born in Nepal and spent five years studying at universities in the USA. He also studied in the Netherlands, England, Norway and India and travelled extensively in Europe. In Nepal he has worked on the English language daily as a journalist and for the planning agency of the Nepalese Government. He has also worked for a year at the United Nations Secretariat in New York and at the OECD in Paris. Prakash has written several books in English and Nepali and also speaks French, German, Spanish and Hindi.

PREVIOUS EDITIONS, THIS EDITION & THE NEXT

The first edition of this Nepal guide was actually published in nepal by Prakash in 1973 with the delightful title 'Nepal on $2 a Day'. Prakash devised his interesting technique of adding short comments from visitors to his country in the first edition and has today interviewed more than 4000 visitors. The first Lonely Planet edition emerged in 1976 and this new edition is the fifth.

Apart from Prakash's work thanks must also go to Peter for the illustrations, Fiona for the new maps and additions to the old ones, Ann for typesetting, Todd for pasting up and proofreading and Michael for editing.

Things change – prices go up, good places go bad, bad places go bankrupt and nothing stays the same. so if you find things better, worse, cheaper, more expensive, recently opened or long ago closed please don't blame us but please do write and tell us about it. As usual the best letters will score a free copy of the next edition or of any other LP guide if you prefer.

The cartoons on page 44-45 and 129 are by Tony Jenkins

Contents

Contents

Introduction

The number of travellers who are tired of travelling to the conventional, tourist infested resorts increases year by year. Among young people especially, there is a genuine yearning for a place which is really different, where the rhythm of life is not as fast, where the way of life is older and less altered by the modern world. With young people Nepal has almost become a legend.

After visiting Kathmandu recently a French writer said:

. . . the traveller starts to realise that the travel agencies have not told him everything. Some have talked of Kathmandu as being situated in the shadow of Everest (which is not true), others have described it as the Mecca of the hippies (which is only half true), but the most important thing has been left unsaid. It has been forgotten to mention that Kathmandu is the Florence of Asia, the city of art par excellence, a wonder of the modern world where Europe of the middle ages can still be discovered.

Perhaps that is why the number of tourists to Nepal is increasing so dramatically.

Nepal has many things to offer to a visitor, such as its unique combination of works of man and nature. The flourishing of art and architecture is amply demonstrated by the temples of the Kathmandu Valley; the beauties of nature by soaring peaks like Mount Everest and others, not so high perhaps, but even more spectacular in appearance.

Nepal is one of the best places in the world for trekking. Not only is trekking comparatively safe but in remote villages every household would consider it its duty to extend hospitality to a weary traveller. Recently, rafting in the rivers originating in the Himalayan glaciers has become very popular. Nor are there many countries in the world where the contrast between old and new is so striking. In the streets of Kathmandu you will see the latest model Japanese cars while only a few minutes away from the capital people cultivate their fields with bullocks. For them things

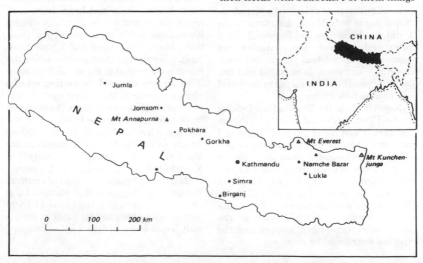

have changed very little in the past five centuries.

The Kathmandu Valley has been called one big museum – a vast storehouse of Hindu and Buddhist art with more shrines and temples per square km than anywhere else in the world. Two hundred years ago, in a statement that still has a wisp of truth in it, the English author Kirkpatrick said:

The valley consists of as many temples as there are houses and as many idols as there are men.

Nor is this a dry, dead museum – Nepal celebrates countless festivals every year and has developed institutions such as the *living goddess* to ensure that this is a living museum. The Nepalese even boast of having developed the pagoda style of architecture and successfully exporting it to China and Japan.

Nepal also contains an amazing mixture of ethnic and racial groups. In the streets of Kathmandu one might think passers-by were Japanese, Chinese, Indonesian, Indian, Arab, Greek or Latin American but it is entirely within the bounds of possibility that they would all be Nepalese. Nepal is the only Hindu kingdom in the world, but Hinduism and Buddhism have co-existed amicably for centuries and many people profess both religions. Buddha's birthplace is in Nepal and one of the largest Buddhist stupas in the world can also be found here.

Nepal is one of the few windows looking on to Tibetan life and culture. Tibetan refugees live in many parts of Nepal and run some excellent restaurants and curio shops in Kathmandu. Near the Chinese border some Nepalse also speak Tibetan. One of the finest wildlife experiences in Asia can now be found in Nepal's Chitwan National Park which is only a few hours from Kathmandu. Such wildlife as the one-horned rhino, tiger, leopard and the spotted deer could be seen.

In terms of per capita income, just US$170 in 1982, Nepal is one of the least developed countries in the world. It was also, until 1973, one of the countries where the smoking of hashish was tolerated – some would even say legal. This was one of the reasons Nepal gained a name as a hippie paradise. Overland travellers consider Kathmandu, with its abundant and varied supply of restaurants, the best place to eat east of Istanbul. As a place to get away from it all and relax at the end of a long trip it can hardly be surpassed. Nor can there be many places in the east where you will run into so many visitors from so many different countries in so small an area.

Nepal is a tiny country, sandwiched between the two largest, in terms of population, in the world – India and China. Perhaps as a result of this it has managed to get substantial foreign aid from the USA, USSR, China, India, the UK, West Germany, Switzerland and Israel to name just a few. The east-west road running the length of Nepal through the southern jungle is divided into sections constructed with assistance from India, the USSR, the UK and the Asian Development Bank. China and India have each aided the construction of roads linking Kathmandu with their respective frontiers. India, China and the USSR have built power generating plants, while the Swiss have helped in the rehabilitation of Tibetan refugees and the setting up of a cheese factory, the Germans in the restoration of ancient temples, the Russians in setting up a cigarette factory, and the Chinese a leather factory. Within walking distance of each other in Kathmandu are libraries opened by the Americans, British, French, Indians, Russians and Chinese.

Nepal is undoubtedly a land of contrast but evidence suggests this Shangri La is changing fast. In 1983, their were 179,000 tourists compared to just 6200 in 1961 – visit Nepal soon, before it is too late.

Facts about the Country

In the course of history the area of Nepal has shrunk and expanded. Sometimes it consisted only of Kathmandu and neighbouring principalities, at other times it extended further east and west from its present boundaries. Nepal's history is a long one. A stone pillar erected more than 2000 years ago by the Indian emperor Ashoka at Lumbini in southern Nepal marks it as the birthplace of the Buddha. During those 2000 years Nepal has seen a steady migration of people speaking Indo-European languages from the western Himalayas and the plains of India on one hand and Mongoloid people speaking Tibeto-Burmese languages from Tibet on the other.

The first known rulers of the Kathmandu Valley were the Kirats who had come from the eastern part of the country. Little is known about these people but one of their kings did rate a mention in the *Mahabharata*, and it was at this time that Buddhism arrived in the country. The Lichhavis came to power from north India during the 4th century AD to the early 7th century. Again comparatively little is known about them but at the temple of Changunarayan a stone inscription can be seen dating from this period.

During the 17th century the three independent, sovereign kingdoms of the Malla dynasty in the Kathmandu Valley created great numbers of works of art, statues and temples. The kingdoms minted their own coins and maintained standing armies. At this time all of what is now Nepal was divided into small principalities and kingdoms. Western Nepal alone had 22 and there were a further 24 in far western Nepal.

From one of these small kingdoms, Gorkha, where kings of the Shah dynasty ruled, King Prithvi Narayan Shah set out to unify Nepal. In 1768 he defeated the Malla kings and Nepal has been ruled by Shah kings ever since. For half a century after 1768 Nepal continued to extend boundaries until in 1817 Nepal lost a war with Britain. As reward for its support during the Indian Mutiny Nepal regained part of its lost territory in 1858 and assumed its present size.

In 1846 Jung Bahadur, Prime Minister of Nepal, took over real power, after the *Kot massacre* where his supporters managed to kill almost all his opponents. For over a century the hereditary family of *Rana* Prime Ministers ruled the country and did very little for development. While almost all the countries of Asia and Africa were being colonised Nepal managed to preserve its independence and was never ruled by a colonial power. Throughout the Rana period Nepal was virtually isolated from the rest of the world. Visitors were rarely admitted and then only with severely circumscribed freedom of movement. In 1951 King Tribhuvan overthrew the Rana regime with support from India. It was a unique situation as the king had led a revolution against an oligarchic system. King Tribhuvan died in 1955 and was succeeded by his son King Mahendra, father of the present king.

Nepal became a member of the United Nations in 1955 and was even elected a member of the Security Council for a two year period in 1969-1970. After a decade of experiments in parliamentary democracy, including elections for parliament in 1958, King Mahendra introduced a system of partyless *Panchayat* democracy in 1962. King Birendra ascended the throne after his father's death in 1972, but his coronation did not take place until an auspicious date in February 1975, three years later, had been selected by astrologers. Many foreign dignitaries attended the colourful coronation ceremony in the historic old royal palace.

King Birendra was educated at Eton in England and Harvard in the US. He is intensely interested in the development of Nepal and the country has made significant progress under his leadership. Nepal has been divided into five development regions: Pokhara (western Nepal), Surkhet (far western Nepal) and Dhankuta (eastern Nepal) are the regional development centres away from Kathmandu. In 1980 a national referendum was held to decide whether to continue with the partyless Panchayat system or to change to a multi-party form of government. The decision went, narrowly, to the Panchayat system although significant changes are expected to be made.

GEOGRAPHY, POPULATION & ECONOMY

Although Nepal is a small country of only 141,577 square km it contains the greatest altitude variation on earth, from the lowland Terai, almost at sea level, to Mt Everest, which at 8848 metres is the highest point on earth. The country is about 800 km long and from 90 to 230 km wide. A cross-section shows four main areas to the country. Close to the border with India is a low fertile strip of jungle land known as the Terai. Until comparatively recently malaria made this an inhospitable region but its eradication has led to a rapid population increase.

Above the Terai rise the Siwalik foothills and beyond them the higher, more barren Mahabharat range. The bulk of the population of Nepal is found in the fertile intermontane valleys, such as the Kathmandu Valley and the Pokhara Valley, north of the Mahabharat range and at altitudes between 1000 and 2000 metres. North again rises the sweep of the Himalayan range forming a barrier between Tibet and Nepal. In general the border runs along the peaks of the range, Mt Everest straddles the border, but in western Nepal at the country's widest point a portion of the high arid Tibetan plateau forms the legendary Mustang province. The Terai also disappears at a point where the Indian border comes right up to the Siwalik foothills.

The population of Nepal is about 16 million and that of Kathmandu, the main city, about 300,000. Like the geography the population of the country is extremely diverse. Some tribes, such as the Sherpas living in the eastern Everest region, have won fame as mountaineers while others, like the Gurungs, Magars and Chetris in the west and the Rais and Limbus in the east have made their mark as Gurkha soldiers. The original inhabitants of the Kathmandu Valley, the Newars, have made significant contributions in the development of art and architecture. Nepalese living in the Terai have close ethnic and linguistic ties with people across the border in the Bihar and Uttar Pradesh states of India.

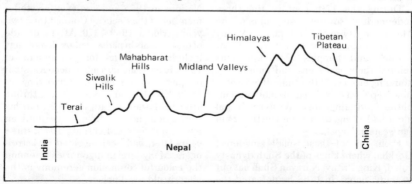

Tamang Girl

Nepal's main exports are rice and jute which are grown in the Terai. Tourism is now superseding the Gurkha earnings as Nepal's chief foreign currency earner. Mineral wealth in Nepal appears to be limited and inaccessible, a result of the country's geological newness. Nepal has vast potential for the development of hydro-electric power.

Development in Nepal is concentrated on improvements in communications, agriculture and education. The road building programme is continuing to link previously isolated parts of the country. In agriculture the green revolution has had a major impact on Nepal, particularly in the fertile but heavily populated Kathmandu Valley which is now able to feed itself. Nevertheless Nepal's steep population growth will continue to put pressure on agricultural potential. Birth control programmes are a major part of the educational development which it is hoped will reduce the illiteracy rate from its current levels of over 70% amongst males and over 90% amongst females. However, 69% of primary school age children are now attending primary school.

In 1982 the average life expectancy was only 46. Much remains to be done to increase the number of hospitals and doctors as there is only one doctor for every 96,000 people. Since most of the doctors are living in Kathmandu, this disparity is even more extreme in the remote areas of the country.

CULTURE & CUSTOMS

Nepal is the meeting place of two great religions, Hinduism and Buddhism; two races, caucasian and mongoloid; and two civilisations, Indic and Sinic. The population has a variety of ethnic groups each with distinct cultural identity.

Polygamy was, and still is, practised in many areas of the country although legislation has banned it in the last decade. In the northern hill areas polyandry, the custom of a wife having more than one husband, was also practised. Ethnic groups such as the Brahmins and Chetris are prohibited from drinking alcohol and sometimes follow vegetarian restraints. Widow remarriage and cousin marriages are not socially acceptable in some groups and amongst Brahmin families a man first meets his wife on the day he gets married. On the other hand the Gurung group have an institution called *Rodighar* intended to bring people together before they contemplate marriage. The Sherpas have a remarkably free and easy moral code.

When going inside rooms in Nepali homes it is polite to remove your shoes. Westerners should not try to enter Hindu temples and never touch the deity although they are quite free to watch from outside. Public displays of affection are not good manners, nor should one swim naked in lakes or rivers. Like many parts of Asia the sight of men and boys walking hand in hand is quite normal and does not have the same connotation it does in the west. Many young Nepalese children have started coming to trekkers and asking for money, this is one of the bad effects of tourism and should not be encouraged. The speed and intensity of change in

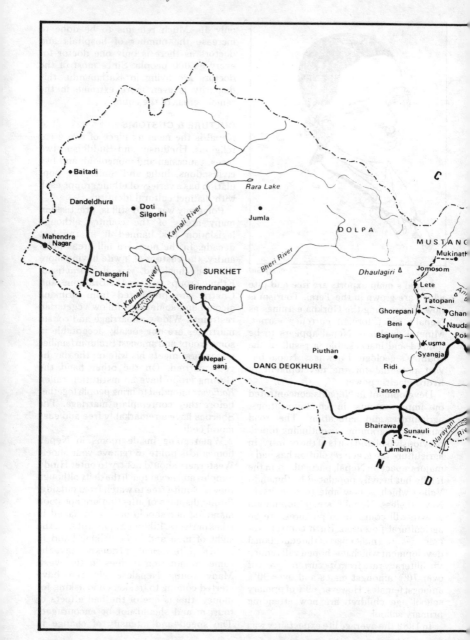

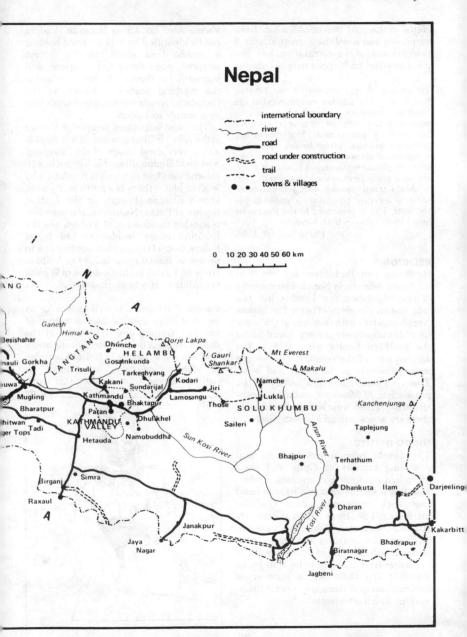

Nepal

- international boundary
- river
- road
- road under construction
- trail
- • towns & villages

0 10 20 30 40 50 60 km

Besishahar
Ganesh Himal
Dhunche
Dorje Lakpa
HELAMBU
Gosainkunda
Mt Everest
Gauri Shankar
Makalu
Trisuli
Tarkeghyang
Kakani
Sundarijal
Kodari
Namche
nauli Gorkha
uwa
Mugling
Kathmandu
Bhaktapur
Jiri
Lukla
Those
SOLU KHUMBU
Kanchenjunga
Bharatpur
Patan
Lamosangu
KATHMANDU
Dhulikhel
VALLEY
hitwan Tadi
Saileri
Taplejung
ger Tops
Hetauda
Namobuddha
Sun Kosi River
Terhathum
Birganj
Simra
Bhajpur
Dhankuta
Ilam
Darjeeling
Raxaul
Dharan
Janakpur
Kosi River
Kakarbitt
Jaya
Nagar
Bhadrapur
Biratnagar
Jagbeni
Arun River
LANGTANG
N A
A

Nepal in the past two decades has been surprising and it will be a great shame if this process of westernisation has too great an effect on Nepal's unique culture.

To anyone deeply interested in Tibetan Buddhism it is a Tibetan custom to visit the Rimpoche (reincarnate lama) of the nearby monastery. Generally the purpose is to receive his blessings and consult him concerning important matters, often to ask questions concerning dharma and sometimes only to take an offering to the monastery. A Khata gift scarf, available at any Tibetan shop for about Rs 1.50 is always taken, usually with a donation of butter or tea or perhaps money wrapped inside the scarf. This is presented to the Rimpoche held loosely between both hands.

Philip Wolcott, USA

RELIGION

Hinduism and Buddhism are the two important religions in Nepal. The majority of the population are Hindus but the religions are closely intertwined and many Nepalese adopt both religions at the same time. Buddhists are mainly found along the northern border area and in the eastern part of the country. Hindus are most numerous in the south and west. There is a small number, about 3% of the population, of Moslems, mainly concentrated along the border with India although there are also scattered Moslem villages.

HINDU DEITIES

The Hindu religion has a large and confusing number of Gods and their attendant consorts and animals. Understanding is simplified if you bear in mind that each represents some God-like attribute. The three main Gods are Brahma the creator, Vishnu the preserver and Shiva the destroyer and regenerator. Brahma, whose consort is Saraswati, is not as revered in Nepal as he is in India. Each of the Gods has a number of incarnations and there are several incarnations which are unique to Nepal.

Vishnu Also known as Narayan, Vishnu can be identified by his four arms holding a *sankha* (sea shell), *chakra* (round weapon), *gada* (stick-like weapon), and *padma* (lotus flower). Vishnu's animal is the mythical man-bird known as the Garuda; a Garuda will often be found close by a temple to Vishnu.

The most important temple of Vishnu in the valley is Changunarayan but there is also a very good image of the 'sleeping' Vishnu at Budhanilkantha. Vishnu has 10 incarnations one of which is Krishna, who is often blue – there is a particularly well-known Krishna Temple in the Durbar Square of Patan. Narsimha, the man-lion is another incarnation of Vishnu, see the beautiful image inside the old Royal Palace. Some Hindus consider Buddha to be one of the 10 incarnations of Vishnu. His wife, Laxmi, is the Goddess of Wealth according to Hindu mythology.

Garuda The Garuda is well known for its aerial abilities and its intense hatred of snakes – Garuda devours snakes at the door of almost all the temples of Kathmandu. You will see a Garuda in front of temples of Vishnu. Indonesia has named its national airline Garuda after this same

Garuda

famous man-bird but the Indonesian Garuda is less man and more bird than the Nepalese variety.

Shiva Pashupatinath, which is another name for the god, is the best known temple to Shiva in the valley. Shiva is often represented by the *lingam* or phallus as a symbol of his creative side. Shiva's animal is the bull, Nandi, and there is a giant sized Nandi in front of Pashupatinath. The image of Pashupatinath itself contains five heads, this is not common in other temples of Shiva. The weapon of Shiva is the *trisul* or trident. According to Hindu mythology Shiva is supposed to live in the Himalayas, smoke a lot of hashish and wear a garland of snakes. Bhairab is a representation of the terrible form of Shiva and there are numerous images of Bhairab in the valley.

Parvati Parvati is the consort of Shiva and like her god she has a peaceful and a fearful side to her activities. She is shown in her terrifying form holding a variety of weapons and her animal is the lion. Dasain, celebrated in her honour, is characterised by the sacrifice of animals. Daxinkali is the best known of her temples.

Hanuman The monkey god Hanuman is the legendary figure from the epic Ramayana who helped rescue Rama's wife Sita from the clutches of the demon Rawana. Rama is yet another of the incarnations of Vishnu and Hanuman was his faithful servant. An image of Hanuman guards the Hanuman Dhoka, entrance to the old Royal Palace of Kathmandu.

Ganesh Easily recognised by his elephant head, Ganesh, the God of Learning, has many temples in Nepal. The animal of Ganesh, which he rides as his 'vehicle', is the mouse! In the course of general worship Ganesh is the first of the deities to be worshipped and the Maru Ganesh temple near Durbar Square in Kathmandu

is visited by a large number of devotees from dawn until late at night.

Shiva, Ganesh's father, is said to have returned to his wife Parvati after a journey lasting 14 years. Arriving home at night he found Parvati asleep with a young boy beside her. Suspecting her of infidelity he immediately lopped off the boy's head and then discovered it was his own son. Shiva was very sad and said he would bring his son back to life if the first living thing seen in the morning was brought to him. The first living thing turned out to be an elephant and Shiva took its head and joined it to the trunk of his son who became Ganesh.

FESTIVALS IN NEPAL

Few people in the world can celebrate as many festivals as the Newars of Kathmandu Valley. Hardly a month passes without a major festival or feast, but the three months from August to October is a real festival season and you're bound to see some picturesque festival if you visit Nepal during that time. Major festivals include:

August

Gai Jatra or Cow Festival Hundreds of garlanded and costumed people walk in a long procession accompanied by cows and crowds of happy people. If there has been a death in the family it is expected that a group consisting of two people, usually a boy and a person dressed as a *sadhu* (saint), and a cow, will be sent to participate in the day-long festival. The curious practice originated from the belief that people who happen to be holding a cow's tail at the moment of death have precedence at the hall of justice!

Krishnasthami The best place to watch the celebrations of Krishna's birthday is at the Krishna temple in Patan. Sacred devotional music is played all night if you can manage to stay awake. Go early in the evening.

Teej This is a special festival for women and all married women are supposed to fast all day and bathe in the holy waters of the rivers. The entrance to Pashupatinath is a good place to watch as crowds of women, dressed in brightly coloured saris with red marks on their foreheads, come down to the river. It is believed that their married life will be long and happy and they will not lose their husbands if they celebrate this festival. Red is a symbol of joy and happiness in Nepal and the colour used for marriage ceremonies. Married women are expected to wear a lot of red but widows are forbidden to do so; white is the colour of mourning in Nepal.

Thousands of women dressed in saris flock to the temple of Pashupatinath on fasting day to do their obeisance to Shiva and his consort Parvati. One or two days later there is a ritual of washing in the holy waters of the Bagmati River in which everyone washes everything 360 times. One can go, unobtrusively, to the more sacred spots on the river bank and witness the marvellous crowds of women singing and joyously cleansing their bodies and souls.

Meg Levine, USA

Unfortunately it's not all sweetness and light at this festival, as this photograph of three western 'gentlemen' illustrates.

I was disgusted to see the behaviour of some tourists at the Shivaratri festival at the Pashupatinath Temple. It is a very holy day for Nepalesé Hindus who come to bathe in the Bagmati River. Millions of pilgrims had made the trip, some sadhus coming from the Punjab and further afield. As I took this photo (with a 135 mm lens) the embarrassment of the Nepali

ladies trying to bathe and pray discreetly was evident. Upon approaching these three quite politely and asking them if they were aware of the discomfort they were causing amongst these women I was told in no uncertain terms to 'F . . . off!'

The Shivaratri festival is a photographers' dream, full of colour and made for fantastic photos of 'the people'. But surely people who travel through these lands must realise after a very short time in the country, if they are at all sensitive to the new cultures they are experiencing, that the local women are generally very camera-shy and certainly when pointing your camera at someone it is obvious whether they approve. Efforts must be made not to upset the locals and make a worse name for tourists in these lands.

Kim Ellis, England

September

Indrajatra The Indra festival, in honour of the ancient Aryan God Indra, God of Rain, marks the end of the monsoon and the beginning of the best season of the year, which lasts for two months. The living goddess, Kumari, is taken in procession through the streets of Kathmandu and the king receives blessings from her. The image of White Bhairab, behind the Black Bhairab in Kathmandu's Durbar Square, is unveiled for three days each year during this festival. Traditional Newar folk dances are performed in the streets around the Durbar Square, Basantapur Square and the Indrachowk area. On this same day, in 1768, King Prithvi Narayan Shah conquered Kathmandu and took the major step in the process of unifying Nepal. The festival continues for four days.

October

Bada Dasain This is the biggest festival in Nepal and lasts 15 days in all although the main festivities are concentrated in nine days during which all schools and government offices are closed. On the seventh day, called 'Fulpati', you can see, around noon or early afternoon, a procession for government officials in national dress preceded by a band from the Royal Palace in Durbar Square. On the ninth day, thousands of goats and buffaloes are sacrificed around noon in the courtyard called 'Kot' behind Durbar Square and a stream of blood flows. Similar sacrifices are made in the temples of goddesses through the country and on this day every household in Nepal eats meat. The tenth day, Bijaya Dashami, is the highlight of the festival and all Hindus and many Buddhists go to the relatives and elders in order to receive a 'tika', which is rice immersed in a red liquid placed on their forehead. On the streets of Kathmandu on this day you will hardly see a person who does not wear this red mark. In late afternoon, if you walk two blocks from Durbar Square to the temple of Naradevi, you can see the Festival of the Sword (Khadga Jatra). This day is supposed to represent the victory of good over evil; according to legend the Goddess Durga killed a demon on this day.

The final day of the festival, a full moon day, is marked by much gambling in some Nepalese households. Dasain is not only the biggest festival but a happy one because the weather is perfect, and the rice is ready to be harvested. It is a pleasant time for walking in the hills which makes the visits to relatives enjoyable. In the villages large swings are set up for the children to play on.

November

Tihar The third and fifth days are the most important of this five-day festival. In western India it is the biggest Hindu festival and in Nepal it is second only to Dasain. On the first day crows, the messengers of death, are honoured and fed. The second day is in honour of dogs, the guardians of the dead and the mount of Bhairab. The third day is set aside for cows as the incarnation of Laxmi. This day is called Deepavali, the festival of lights, and all the households of Kathmandu are illuminated by lamps to the Goddess of Wealth. This festival always falls on a new moon so the effect is particularly delightful.

It is said that the Goddess Laxmi will shun any household not illuminated on this day, which is also an occasion for gambling.

The new year for the Newars of the valley also starts from this day. The Nepalese national new year starts on 13 April and 1983 in western terms is 2040 in Nepalese. The Newari calendar equates 1983 to 1103. The Tibetans living in Nepal also have their own calendar.

The fifth day of the festival is Bhai Tika and is meant especially for brothers and sisters who are supposed to get together on this day. There is a small ceremony and they mark each others foreheads with *tikas*. The sister also puts oil on her brother's forehead and offers sweets and fruits, in return he pays her small sums of money, say Rs 5 or 10. On this day the bazaars of Kathmandu are full of sweets and fresh and dry fruits.

Ekadashi On the eleventh day after the new moon Vishnu is supposed to wake up after having slept for four months. There will be many pilgrims at Pashupatinath but the best place to view this festival is at the temple of Changunarayan or at the temple of the sleeping Vishnu at Budhanilkantha. The activities of Budhanilkantha are equally interesting on the next day when a long line of devotees queue to touch the feet of the deity.

December

Bala Chaturdashi People come from all over the valley and beyond to the temple of Pashupatinath to take part in a ceremony which consists of scattering seeds of different kinds and burning candles in memory of their dead relatives. The evening is the best time to observe the ceremony as you will see many pilgrims performing religious rites and singing and dancing. The best place to watch is from across the Bagmati River which gives a good view of the illuminated temple and pilgrims worshipping. Many pilgrims from far away villages spend the night around the temple.

February

Tibetan New Year There are religious celebrations in Bodhnath Stupa around noontime and the Buddhist monks give blessings. This festival is essentially a family affair when friends and members of the family get together.

Maha Shivaratri The birthday of Lord Shiva usually falls in the cold month of February but many pilgrims come from the warm weather of the Terai or the north Indian plains to worship at the temple of Pashupatinath in a colourful yet deeply serene ceremony.

During the festival of Shivaratri, the most impressive feature was the mass of colour and simple dignity of the pilgrims as they performed the ritual bathing in the holy river. Some Sadhus covered with ashes lay on a bed of thorns and also impaled their tongues with thorns.

John Hayward, England

March

Holi or Fagu This festival of rejoicing occurs in the springtime on the day of the full moon in the Nepalese month of Falgun when a pillar is installed in Basantapur Square in front of the old Royal Palace. The festival used to last for eight days and was marked by throwing coloured water and red powder on acquaintances and even people passing by on the street. The festival now takes place only on the day of the full moon but visitors should watch out for the coloured water. If you happen to be on the Helambu trek the village of Tarkeghyang has a colourful festival celebrated with dancing and singing until the late hours. The Sherpas on the mountains do without the water throwing.

April

Chaitra Dasain Also called small Dasain in contrast to October's big Dasain, this festival is similar in many respects, and many goats and buffaloes are sacrificed to the Goddess Durga at the Kot Square. An image of the Goddess is pulled on a chariot through the streets.

Bisket Festival A wooden pillar is erected in the evening on the first day of this Bhaktapur festival. On the second day, which is also the first day of the year by the Nepalese calendar, a chariot is pulled from the pillar to the temple of Bhairabnath in the same square as the five-storey Nyatapola Pagoda. The chariot is very old and looks on the point of collapse – as it is pulled every part shakes violently and it makes a tremendous spectacle. The pillar is shaken violently in the evening and then lowered with great rejoicing. The chariots of Ganesh and the goddess Mahakali and Mahalaxmi are carried on the shoulders of the devotees.

The festival, in fact, consists of a series of festivals lasting for a week which start around 8 April. It's interesting to visit Bhaktapur during any day of the week, but some days are more interesting than others.

May

Birthday of Buddha Since Nepal is the birthplace of Buddha and there are still many Buddhists amongst the Nepalese, this festival is celebrated with especial pomp. Swayambhunath and Bodhnath are particularly popular centres and pilgrims will gather at Swayambhunath from early in the morning.

Rato Machhendranath The festival of Red Machhendranath takes place in Patan over a period of two months and is one of the most complex festivals. During the celebrations a chariot bearing the image of Machhendranath, revered by Hindus and Buddhists, moves in a series of daily stages through the streets of Patan.

July

Naga Panchami Images of the serpent Naga are stuck over the doors of houses during the festival of snakes. Since snakes are believed to have power over the monsoon rainfall, it is important that they are appeased – their image also keeps evil from entering the home

Janai Purnima All high caste Hindus wear a sacred thread over their left shoulder and tied under their right armpit. On this day each year the sacred thread is replaced after a day-long fast. Kumbheswara temple in Patan and the holy lake of Gosainkund are important places for this festival.

Two times a month, on the eleventh day after the full moon and the new moon, a concert of classical Indian music is given in the Narayan Temple very near the new Royal Palace. The best Nepalese musicians, especially tabla and sitar, and several singers of all ages will sing in the evening.

Nadine Beautheac, France

Marriage Ceremony

Marriage ceremonies in Nepal are supposed to take place only in five months of the year – mid-January to mid-March, mid-April to mid-June and mid-November to mid-December. Astrologers select auspicious dates within these periods on the basis of the positions of the stars. It is quite common to see several marriage processions on the same particularly auspicious date. The marriage ritual differs in the various communities but almost always has a procession preceded by a band. The bridegroom spends a night at the bride's house where a big religious ceremony is held during which the bride and groom walk around a fire on a platform so that the fire 'witnesses' their marriage.

FESTIVAL CALENDAR

Almost all of the festivals in Nepal are celebrated according to the lunar calendar so it is difficult to tell in advance the exact dates when they will take place. The festival calendar, made after consulting the lunar calendar, covers major festivals for 1985, 1986 and 1987.

Name of Festival	Place	1985	1986	1987
Bisketjatra – Festival of Bisket	Bhaktapur	13 Apr	14 Apr	13 Apr
Buddha Jayanti – Birthday of Buddha	Kathmandu		23 May	13 May
Gaijatra – Cow Festival	Kathmandu	13 Aug	20 Aug	10 Aug
Krishnasthami – Birthday of Krishna	Patan	7 Sep	27 Aug	16 Aug
Teej – Festival of Women	Pashu-patinath	17 Sep	7 Sep	27 Aug
Indrajatra – Festival of Indra	Kathmandu	27 Sep	17 Sep	6 Sep
Bijaya Dashami – Big Dasain	nationwide			
Navami	"	21 Oct	11 Oct	1 Oct
Tika	"	22 Oct	12 Oct	2 Oct
Tihar – Festival of Light	"	12 Nov	1 Nov	22 Oct
Bhai Tika	"	14 Nov	3 Nov	24 Oct
Big Ekadashi	Kathmandu	22 Nov	12 Nov	2 Nov
Bala Chaturdashi	Pashupat-inath	11 Dec	30 Nov	20 Nov
Basantra Panchami	Swayam-bhunath		13 Feb	3 Feb
Sivaratri – Birthday of Shiva	Pashupat-inath		9 Mar	26 Mar
Holi – Festival of Colour	nationwide		25 Mar	15 Mar
Ghodejatra – Festival of Horse Racing	Kathmandu		9 Apr	29 Mar
Chaitra Dasain	Kathmandu, Gorkha		17 Apr	6 Apr
Tibetan New Year	Bodhnath		Feb	Feb
Mani Rimdu	Solu Khumbu		Nov	11 Nov

LANGUAGE

English is understood by many people in Kathmandu and Pokhara. The national language, Nepali, is related to Hindi and belongs to the Indo-European family of languages; it is a fairly easy language to learn. Many of the Nepalese ethnic groups speak their own language – the Newars of the Kathmandu Valley speak Newari, and distinct languages are spoken by the Gurungs, Magars, Rais, Limbus, Tamangs and Sherpas. In the Terai, Hindu and Maithili are widely spoken and understood.

Although learning a few words of Nepali is a good idea and widely appreciated there is one word every visitor should learn – *Namaste*. This universal Nepalese greeting translates literally as 'I salute all divine qualities in you' but is used as 'hello, how are you, pleased to see you, see you again' and is generally a nice thing to say.

Some useful words

how much?	*kati?*
less	*kam*
where?	*kata?*
OK	*theek*
thank you	*dhanyabad*
more	*badhi*
little bit	*alikati*
that's enough	*pugyo*
I do not have	*chhaina*
good, pretty	*ramro*
here	*yaha*
there	*tyaha*
today	*aaja*
yesterday	*hijo*
tomorrow	*bholi*
stamp	*ticket*
envelope	*kham*
money	*paisa*
cheap	*sasto*
expensive	*mahango*

On the trail

way, trail	*bate*
bridge	*pool*
descent	*oralo*
ascent	*ukalo*
left	*baya*
right	*daya*
cold	*jado*

give me	*malai dinos*
wait a minute	*ek chhin parkhanos*
I like this	*malai yo ramro lagyo*
I do not like this	*malai yo ramro lagena*
where is the market?	*bazar kata parchha?*
where is the road to?	*jane bato kata parchha?*
I do not feel good	*malai sancho chhaina*
is there a village nearby?	*najikai gaun parchha?*
where is the porter?	*bhariya kata gayo?*
please give me tea	*malai chiya dinos*
I want to sleep	*malai sutna man lagyo*
I feel cold	*malai jado lagyo*
I do not need it	*malai chahinna*
I do not have it	*ma sanga chhaine*

Food Words

food	*khana*
boiled	*umaleko*
vegetable	*tarkari*
sugar	*chini*
tomato	*golbeda*
meat	*masu*
bread	*pauroti*
salt	*noon*
pepper	*marich*
water	*pani*
rice	*bhat*
tea	*chiya*
spicy	*peero*
egg	*phool*

chicken	*kukhura*	twenty	*bees*
milk	*doodh*	thirty	*tees*
curd	*dahi*	forty	*chalis*
tastes good	*meetho chha*	fifty	*pachas*
		sixty	*sathi*
Numbers		seventy	*sattari*
		eighty	*assi*
one	*ek*	ninety	*nabbey*
two	*dui*	one hundred	*saya*
three	*teen*	two hundred	*dui saya*
four	*char*	five hundred	*panch saya*
five	*panch*	one thousand	*hazar*
six	*chha*	one hundred-	*lakh*
seven	*sat*	thousand	
eight	*sath*	one million	*das lakh*
nine	*nau*	ten million	*crore*
ten	*das*		

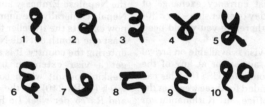

1 2 3 4 5

6 7 8 9 10

Facts for the Visitor

VISAS

Nepal has embassies or consular offices in most European countries, the USA and in most of its Asian neighbours. Overland travellers generally collect their Nepalese visas in Bangkok or Calcutta if westbound; in New Delhi if travelling east.

Visas cost US$10 or equivalent and are valid for 30 days. Further extensions, up to a maximum of three months cost Rs 75 per week (or Rs 300 per month) for the second month, and Rs 150 per week (or Rs 600 per month) for the third month. When extending visas it is necessary to provide proof of official currency exchange of US$5 for each day of extension – for a 30-day extension therefore you would need US$150.

A seven-day visa is available on arrival at Kathmandu airport or at any of the border entry points for US$10. This can be further extended for three weeks at the immigration office in Kathmandu or Pokhara at no cost.

The immigration offices (tel 4-12337) at Maiti Devi in Kathmandu, or near the lake in Pokhara, extend visas and also issue trekking permits. Local police offices can also extend visas for up to seven days at a time. Nepalese visas are endorsed as being valid only in and around the Kathmandu and Pokhara Valleys and at Chitwan. This permits travel along all the major roads and short treks around the valley. If you intend to take a longer trek you must obtain a trekking permit for the route you intend to walk. Trekking permits are only available in Kathmandu and Pokhara and can only be extended in these cities. Besides, police offices in any district can also extend trekking permits for a week. The Immigration Office in Kathmandu accepts applications till 2 pm and returns the permits before 6 pm on the same day.

It is possible to get visas for longer than three months by studying, teaching or undertaking research work at the university or any institution recognised by the government. Recent practice has made it easier to extend visas for an additional month after the three month limit has expired. This is given by the Ministry of Home on the recommendation of immigration. But you must have a good reason for applying – waiting for money to arrive, intending to watch a festival to be celebrated a month later, etc. Many foreigners go to India after their visa has expired, obtain a new one-month visa at the Nepalese Embassy and then re-enter Nepal. Generally the immigration office now expects the traveller to have spent at least one month outside Nepal before re-entering the country. It is also possible to get a visa extension by obtaining a trekking permit which costs Rs 60 per week (ie Rs 240) for the second month, and Rs 75 per week (ie Rs 300) for the third month. It is therefore cheaper to extend visas by getting a trekking permit and going trekking. Although you do not have to go trekking, immigration does sometimes check to see if you have actually gone. If caught you might be made to pay the difference that you would have paid had you applied for an extension without a trekking permit and a late fee of Rs 10 per day. And if you're found to be trekking without a permit in a restricted area, which includes most of the northern districts (including Dolpo), you may be taken back to Kathmandu and deported immediately.

If travelling to India after Nepal, the practice of not requiring visas for Commonwealth citizens has been changed. All nationalities now require visas to enter India.

Nepalese Diplomatic Offices

Australia
   3/87C Cowles Rd, Mosman, NSW 2088 (tel 02 960 3565)
France
   7 Rue Washington, Paris 75008 (tel 359 2861)
West Germany
   53 Bad Godesberge im Haag, Bonn 2 (tel 34 3097)
India
   1 Barakhamba Rd, New Delhi (tel 38 1484)
   19 Woodlands, Sterndale Rd, Alipur, Calcutta (tel 45 2024)
Thailand
   189 Soi 71, Sukhumvit Rd, Bangkok (tel 391 7240)
UK
   12A Kensington Place Gardens, London W8 (tel 229 6231)
USA
   2131 Leroy Place NW, Washington DC 20008 (tel 667 4550)
Nepalese UN Mission
   820 Second Avenue, Room 1200, New York, NY 10017 (tel 370 4188)

OTHER PAPERWORK
An international driving permit is worth having if there is any chance you may be driving. Experienced budget travellers do not need to be told how useful an International Student Identity Card can be – if you can get one do. If you are youth hostelling then YHA membership may be worth having – there is a youth hostel in Patan in the Kathmandu valley. If you are travelling elsewhere in the region you'll find many in India and in south-east Asia. It's always worth carrying a stack of photos for visa applications, trekking permits and so on. You won't find western-style coin-in-the-slot photo booths in Nepal of course, but Kathmandu's photo studios will do good quality passport photos at way below western prices. There is also a studio opposite the Immigration Office which can develop black and white photos in a few hours. Health insurance is a wise investment. If you take out trekking insurance make sure

it covers helicopter rescue services as well – being flown out by helicopter is not cheap!

HEALTH
A number of vaccinations are highly advisable both for your own safety and for regulations governing return to your own country, although they may not all be required for entry to Nepal. Diseases to avoid include:

Smallpox Vaccination lasts three years but if your current immunisation is getting old re-vaccination is a good idea. Just a painless scratch.
Cholera Another important immunisation, usually given as two injections spaced two weeks apart and valid for six months.
Typhoid and Paratyphoid Also highly recommended, this can be given with the cholera shot as TAB.
Tetanus Since the TAB shot can also immunise against tetanus as TABT, this is a worthwhile extra precaution.
Malaria Particularly if you are visiting the Terai during the wet season, malarial prophylactics are advisable. The usual procedure is a weekly chloroquine tablet or a daily dose of paludrine. In either case start taking the tablets before you arrive in Nepal and continue for two weeks after departure. Malaria has been virtually eradicated from the low lying Terai but care is still advisable.
Hepatitis The best protection against this infectious disease is to take care to eat and drink only clean food and drinks. Gamma globulin injections have a limited and doubtful efficacy and should be taken as closely as possible to your departure.

Your doctor will record immunisations in your International Certificate of Vaccination which must then be stamped by your local health department. With a little care there is no reason for anyone to catch anything in Nepal. Nepalese pharmacies stock a reasonable range of western pharmaceuticals including aspirin (useful for high altitude headaches of trekking) and cough syrup which are often necessary in the cold dry winter air).

MEDICAL FACILITIES

The government hospital in Kathmandu, known as the Bir Hospital (tel 2-11119), is modern and does cholera and typhoid vaccinations and issues international health cards. The Santa Bhawan Mission Hospital was closed recently but the new Patan Hospital (tel 5-22266, 5-22276, 5-22286) also receives assistance from western missionaries. It is located in the Lagankhel area of Patan, near the last stop of the Lagankhel bus. In Pokhara, the former Shining Hospital run by the missionaries has now been merged with Gandaki Zonal Hospital and has facilities which are adequate for Pokhara.

There is a Japanese-trained Nepalese dentist named Dr Mesh Bahadur (tel 2-12282) just behind the fire station in New Rd. His clinic hours are 5 to 7 pm.

The clinic of Dr LN Prasad (tel 2-11801), an eye, ear, nose and throat specialist, is near the National Theatre in Jamal. There is a pathology laboratory opposite the American Library in New Road which is open in the evenings. Gamma globulin shots can be obtained at the Kalimati clinic (tel 2-14743) for Rs 65.

Many westerners interested in Ayurvedic medicine have found Dr Mana (tel 2-13960) to be good. Some even claim he has cured them of hepatitis! His clinic is situated on a street near the Bir Hospital.

CLIMATE & WHEN TO VISIT

October-November and February-March-April are the best times to visit Nepal. In October and November the weather is excellent, neither too hot, nor too cold. As it is immediately after the monsoon there are no clouds or dust in the atmosphere and visibility is extremely good; the Himalayan range will be clearly visible. Rice is harvested in Nepal during these months and two of the biggest festivals

also take place – the Nepalese people will be in a happy and festive mood. This is also the best time for trekking.

In the February to April period the weather is still excellent but due to dust in the air visibility is not quite so good. On the other hand if you go trekking you can see the blooming of flowers at high altitudes especially Nepal's brilliant rhododendrons. The weather in mid-winter, December and January, is still fine and clear but it can be quite cool especially at high altitude where nights can be exceedingly bitter.

The monsoon lasts from the second week of June to the first week of October and this is not the best time to visit the country – although it will be cool and pleasant compared to the plains of India. Trekking is impossible during this season as the trails are slippery and difficult to walk on, rivers may be impassible and Nepal's horrendous leeches will be out waiting for you. Roads can also be blocked at this time due to landslides and the Himalayan peaks are rarely visible due to the constant cloud cover. However many festivals are celebrated in Kathmandu during the second half of the monsoon (August-September) which may make your stay rewarding.

If you visit Nepal in this period a one-week stay in Kathmandu should be adequate with just a short visit out of the valley. If you come in the dry season from October to June a two to four-week stay is better. A week can easily be spent in and around the Kathmandu Valley followed by a week's stay in Pokhara including a short trek. If you have time, a 10-day trek can be made to Ghodepani or Ghandruk from Pokhara or to Helambu from Kathmandu. The long trek to the Everest Base Camp can even be squeezed into two weeks if you fly back to Kathmandu from Lukla.

Maximum summer temperatures in Kathmandu approach 30°C and even at the height of winter a daily maximum approaching 20°C can be expected. Night temperatures in mid-winter can fall to nearly freezing point, 0°C, but it never actually snows in the valley. Pokhara is generally somewhat hotter due to its lower altitude. Nepal's great altitude variations make for some considerable climatic variations from the summer heat on the lowland Terai to the intense cold of the high Himalayas in winter. The Himalayas in Nepal are about 1500 km nearer to the equator than the European Alps – one of the reasons the snow line is so much higher. Apart from the brief winter monsoon, lasting just a day or two in late January, all the rain falls during the monsoon. The lack of precipitation in the winter is another reason for the high snow line, the mountains usually have more snow during the summer.

MONEY

The Nepalese unit of currency is the Rupee which is divided into 100 paisa. There are approximately 17 Nepalese Rupees to the US dollar. Indian and Nepalese Rupees are freely convertible and 100 Indian Rs equals 145 Nepalese Rs. You get a better rate for travellers' cheques than cash. At the time of going to press the official exchange rates in Nepal were:

US$1	= Rs	18
DM1	= Rs	6
A$1	= Rs	15
100 I Rs	= Rs	145

Nepalese currency consists of:
Coins of 5, 10, 25, 50 paisa
Banknotes of 1, 5, 10, 50, 100, 500, 1000 rupees.

The major banks in Nepal are located in New Road. There is a big Nepal Bank building near the statue and park which is open from 10 am to 2 pm on Sundays to Thursdays and from 10 am to 12 noon on Fridays. There is also an office of the Rashtriya Bank located on the first floor of the supermarket. The Rashtriya Bank also has an exchange office in the Thamel area of Kathmandu. Most travellers' cheques can be exchanged at these offices or, usually for resident guests only, at the main hotels. Unlike many other countries, the exchange rate in hotels is identical to the banks. It is wise to get some of your money in smaller rupee denominations. The Rs 100 notes may be difficult to change, particularly in the hills if you go trekking.

Upon entry to Nepal visitors are given a currency exchange card which they are advised to have filled and stamped each time they change money or travellers' cheques. If not, get one from a bank, but don't expect to change $ back. When leaving the country you can re-exchange Nepalese currency providing the amount does not exceed 10% of the total changed or the last amount changed – whichever is greater. There is an exchange counter in the international terminal of the airport.

There is a bank office in Pokhara and money changers operate at border points such as Birganj. Elsewhere in the country you could expect to have difficulty changing travellers' cheques although US dollars can still be changed in major towns. It is advisable to carry sufficient Nepalese currency when trekking to last the whole trek. Until comparatively recently paper money was almost unknown outside the Kathmandu Valley. Mountaineering expeditions in the 1950s would have to have several porters simply to carry the operating money for the expedition and porters' wages – in coins! Several books on expeditions in Nepal speak of the proud swagger of the porter entrusted with carrying half his weight in cash.

Getting Money Sent to Kathmandu

This might involve long delays unless you choose the right bank and do it properly. Many of the major banks in the west (ie Westpac in Australia, Standard Chartered Bank in the UK, Chase Manhattan in the USA) are correspondent banks of the Nepal Bank. The head office is located near the park in New Rd. Money can be sent by telex or other means to Nepal and you can then collect it from the bank. Be as specific as possible when having money transferred internationally and if possible arrange that you yourself are notified when money is transferred as well as the bank.

Recently, CITIBANK based in New York has opened a branch in Kathmandu. Their offices are located in the Yak and Yeti Hotel (tel 4-10884).

GENERAL INFORMATION
Working Days
Saturday is an inauspicious day and most shops and all offices and banks will be closed. Sunday is a regular working day.

Time
Nepalese time is 5 hours 40 minutes ahead of GMT, noon in London is 5.40 pm in Kathmandu. The odd 10 minutes is intended to differentiate Nepal from India which is 5 hours 30 minutes ahead of GMT.

What to Wear
During most of the year light summer clothes are all you'll need in Kathmandu and the valley. An umbrella is a vital addition during the monsoon and in the depths of winter you'll want a sweater during the day and a warm coat at night. In the mountains, even in mid-winter, the days will be warm but the nights bitterly cold. The burning power of the sun at high altitudes is phenomenal – sunglasses and covering unprotected skin are advisable.

Film and Camera
Although Kathmandu has a number of camera shops, obtaining film is both expensive and difficult. What film there is available has usually been sold by visitors and is of doubtful age and quality. If you are using an SLR camera a telephoto lens is a virtual necessity for good mountain close-ups when trekking. Remember also to allow for the exceptional intensity of mountain light when setting exposures at high altitude. Most Nepalese people are quite happy to be photographed but they may demand baksheesh for posing. Sherpa people are an exception and can be very camera shy.

Electricity
Electric current, when available, is 220 volts/50 cycles throughout Nepal – American 120 volt electrical items will require a transformer.

Tipping
Tipping is not a normal practice in Nepal so don't make it one. Taxi drivers certainly don't expect to be tipped nor do budget hotels and restaurants. Only in the more expensive establishments will there be a 10% service charge added to your bill.

Police
The police phone number is 2-11999.

Airline Offices
Air France, Annapurna Hotel Arcade, Durbar Marg (tel 2-13339)
Air India, Kantipath, Kantipath (tel 2-12335)
Bangladesh Biman*, Durbar Marg (tel 2-12544)
British Airways, Durbar Marg (tel 2-12266)
Burma Airways Corporation*, Durbar Marg (tel 14839)
Indian Airlines*, Durbar Marg (tel 2-14839)
Japan Airlines, Trans Himalayan Trekking, Durbar Marg (tel 2-13854)
KLM, Ghorkha Travels, Durbar Marg (tel 2-14896)
Lufthansa, Annapurna Hotel Arcade, Durbar Marg (tel 2-13896)
Pakistan International Airlines*, Durbar Marg (tel 2-13052)
Pan American, Durbar Marg (tel 2-15824)
Royal Nepal Airlines*, New Road (tel 2-14511)
Thai International*, Durbar Marg (tel 2-14387, 2-13565)
SAS, c/o Thai International
TWA, Kantipath (tel 2-14704)

fly to Nepal

Postal Services

The Kathmandu GPO is on the corner of Kantipath and Khichapokhari close to the Bhimsen Tower and opens from 10 am to 5 pm daily; a small stamp counter opens earlier. There is a separate International Post Office for parcels and a Telecommunications Office both situated quite close to the GPO. The Poste Restante counter is in the GPO and is quite efficient. But as with any other Asian country you are advised to ask that your surname is printed clearly and underlined if you are having mail sent to the Poste Restante. There is also a post office counter at the airport.

Postal Rates

	Afr, Eur	Aus, US
Aerograms	3.50	4
Postcards	3	3
Letter/20 gm	6.25	7
Registration	6	6

Government Offices

Immigration and other government offices are open from 10 am to 5 pm from Sunday to Friday and from 10 am to 4 pm during the three winter months.

Government Tourist Office

The tourist office on Ganga Path opposite Basantapur Square (tel 2-11203) has a large variety of brochures and maps and shows films on Nepal.

Travel Agencies

Annapurna Travels, Durbar Marg (tel 2-13940)
Continental Travels & Tours, Durbar Marg (tel 2-14299)
Everest Travel Service, Ganga Path (tel 2-15392)
Euerest Express Travels, Durbar Marg (tel 2-16769)
Gorkha Travels, Durbar Marg (tel 2-14895)
Himalayan Travels & Tours, Jamal (tel 2-11682)
Kathmandu Tours & Travels, Dharma Path (tel 2-14446)
Malla Travels, Kantipath (tel 4-10635)
Natraj Travels & Tours, Durbar Marg (tel 2-15021)
President Travel & Tours, Durbar Marg (tel 2-15021)
Pokhara Tours & Travel, New Road (tel 14613)
Shankar Travels & Tours, Shankar Hotel, Lazimpat (tel 4-11465)
Yangrima Tours, Tripureshwar (tel 2-15814)
Yeti Travels, Durbar Marg (tel 12329 & 11234)

Trekking Agencies

Annapurna Mountaineering and Trekking, Durbar Marg (tel 2-12736)
Lama Excursions, Durbar Marg (tel 2-15840)
Mountain Travels, Box 170, Kathmandu (tel 4-14508)
Sherpa Co-Operative Trekking, Kamal Pokhari (tel 2-15887)
Great Himalayan Adventure, Kantipath (tel 2-16144)
Sherpa Trekking Service, Kamaladi (tel 2-12489)
Yangri Treks, Tripureshwar (tel 2-16144)

Foreign Embassies

Australia, Baluwatar (tel 4-11578)
Burma, Pulchowk (tel 5-21788)
China (PRC), Baluwatar (tel 4-12589)
Egypt, Jawlakhel (tel 5-21844)
Federal Republic of Germany, Kantipath (tel 2-11730)
France, Lazimpat (tel 4-12332)
Great Britain, Lainchaur (tel 2-11588)
India, Lainchaur (tel 2-11300)
Israel, Bishramalaya-Lazimpat (tel 2-11251)
Italy, Baluwatar (tel 4-12743)
Japan, Lazimpat (tel 2-12730)
Pakistan, Ranipokhari (tel 11431)
Thailand, Thapathali (tel 2-13912)
UNDP, Lainchaur (tel 2-16444)
USA, Panipokhari (tel 2-11255)

Getting There

ENTERING NEPAL BY LAND

It is possible to enter Nepal by land via three main routes. Most of the 20% of foreign visitors who arrive in Nepal by these land routes are overlanders making the trans-Asian trip from Europe. If you are travelling by Indian train this is a very cheap way of getting to Nepal but it can also be very slow. The trains running up to the Indian border towns travel on *metre gauge* instead of the much faster *broad gauge* lines, as is the case between Delhi and Calcutta. It is faster and more convenient to take a bus from Muzaffarpur or Gorakhpur to the border.

The most popular land entries are from Sunauli near Lumbini, north of the Indian city of Gorakhpur, then by road to Kathmandu via Narayanghat or to Pokhara directly. As Kathmandu is now only seven hours away by express bus from Sunauli, anyone travelling from Delhi or Varanasi will find it more convenient to enter from Sunauli. On the other hand, those travelling from Calcutta or Patna will enter Nepal from Raxaul and will travel to Kathmandu via Narayanghat. Because of the opening of the connecting road from Narayanghat to Mugling on the Pokhara-Kathmandu road there are now very few buses using the old Rajpath, constructed by India in the 1950s. However, the Rajpath (from Hetaura to Naubise along the Birganj-Kathmandu route) is more scenic and has some beautiful spots to view the Himalaya in the autumn. There is also a third possible entrance route to Nepal, at Kakarbitta in the east, near Darjeeling.

The road from Birganj was constructed with Indian assistance in the late 1950s and named Tribhuvan Rajpath after the late King Tribhuvan. The Sunauli to Pokhara road was also built by the Indians but in the late sixties. It is named the Siddhartha Highway after Buddha whose birthplace at Lumbini is near its Indian starting point. Siddhartha is another name for Buddha. The road between Pokhara and Kathmandu was constructed with Chinese assistance in the early seventies.

During the monsoon, the road from Sunauli to Pokhara may be closed for a few days by landslides. However, the road to Kathmandu via Narayanghat and Mugling is unlikely to remain closed due to its economic importance. The eastern route from Darjeeling may also be susceptible to monsoon blockages in which case it would be necessary to travel by train from Siliguri to Raxaul before entering Nepal. Soon (perhaps) before the end of 1986), it may be possible to travel overland between Nepal and the Tibet region of China by the overland route. Although the road is not yet open officially to travel for westerners, I met more than a dozen western travellers in early 1985 who had travelled overland from Lhasa to Kathmandu. It might be worthwhile to check to get the latest information.

TO KATHMANDU FROM SUNAULI

Sunauli on the Indo-Nepal border can be reached by a Rs 13 bus ride from the city of Gorakhpur. If you want to visit Lumbini, Buddha's birthplace, you should make an overnight stay in the city of Bhairawa. If not you can get buses heading directly to either Kathmandu or Pokhara.

Sunauli is just Rs 55 and a seven-hour bus ride from Kathmandu. Buses leave either early in the morning or at 1 pm. There are also night buses but you are not advised to take them unless you want to miss the views or want to be in a bus driving in the mountains in the night. The bus passes through Bhairawa and then the city of Butwal, in the Siwalik hills, the outermost of the Himalayan ranges. Here you turn east on the East-West Highway.

This sector from Butwal to Narayanghat was constructed with British aid in the 1970s. For two hours you roll across the plains of the Terai, before crossing a small hill at Barghat where you enter the intermontane valley known as the 'Inner Terai'.

You then cross the River Narayani, one of Nepal's three biggest rivers, and reach the town of Narayanghat. This is the main town of the rich agricultural area known as Chitwan. Chitwan is also the name of the national park famed for its rhinoceros and the game reserve is only a couple of hours drive from this city. From Narayanghat the bus follows the Trisuli River north to Mugling at the Pokhara-Kathmandu Highway. From here you drive through the towns like Benighat and Gajuri before reaching a fertile valley where guavas and sugar are grown. The road finally crosses a ridge and descends into the valley.

TO KATHMANDU FROM RAXAUL

A three rupee rickshaw ride will take you from the Indian border town of Raxaul to the town of Birganj. As there are many night service buses available it is not necessary to overnight here but you may like to take a bus during the daytime to watch the scenary. Almost all of the cheap lodges are found around the bus station. Birganj is not really a very pleasant place to stay but you don't really have much choice in the matter! See the Terai section for more details on this small border town.

The buses to Kathmandu leave between 6 am and 9 am in the morning and charge Rs 40, knock off 20% if you hold an International Student ID card. If you can find a spare seat in a truck you can travel for Rs 25 to 30. Or you can go by more comfortable minibus for Rs 44 and enjoy a better view of the surroundings. Several bus companies operate this route, some of the better ones include *Sajha*. Try not to get a seat over the bus wheelbase, and those right at the back also give an uncomfortable ride.

Birganj has a population of about 30,000. A sugar factory and an agricultural implements factory have been constructed here with Russian assistance. The Tribhuvan Rajpath runs 200 km from Birganj to Kathmandu and reaches a maximum altitude of over 2500 metres. Although the scenery is very spectacular most people prefer not to make this trip too often, it takes over eight hours by bus and is extremely tiring due to the constant ups, downs and arounds. In a car the time could be cut to five hours.

North of Birganj you can see the heavily forested Siwalik Hills. The southernmost and youngest mountains in Nepal. The almost treeless Mahabharat range is visible beyond and if the weather is clear the main Himalayan range can be seen still further to the north. The road from Birganj runs through the flatlands known as the Terai as far as the town of Amlekhganj. The people in this area have close linguistic ties with India but since the eradication of malaria in the Terai during the 1960s there has been much migration from the hill country. Eleven km before reaching the foothills the road passes through a dense sal forest.

From Amlekhganj the road climbs over the Siwalik hills then descends to Hetaura, the biggest town between Birganj and Kathmandu. Situated in the rich intermontane Rapti Valley this town is the regional administrative headquarters and has a small industrial estate where Nepal's first brewery produces Star Beer with German assistance. In the 1920s, long before the road was constructed, an aerial ropeway was built between Kathmandu and Hetaura. It still carries goods to this day. If you wish to make an overnight stay at Hetaura the *Hotel Rapti* charges Rs 40 for a single with bath.

After Hetaura you enter the Chitwan Valley, well known both as an agricultural region and as the home of the Royal Game Reserve and the Chitwan National Park. If you are interested in wildlife you can make a stopover in Tandi Bazaar, en route to

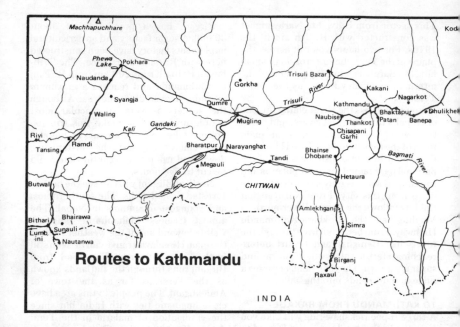

Routes to Kathmandu

Narayanghat, and stay overnight in one of the hotels or cheap lodges.

Before the construction of the road from Narayanghat to Mugling, buses would continue from Hetaura directly north to Kathmandu. Bhainse is beyond Hetaura and from here you travel through the Mahabharat range and soon reach the highest point known as Sim Bhanjyang. A few km away at Daman, 80 km before Kathmandu, there is a view tower at 2300 metres from where you can see an incredible view of the entire Himalayan range in Nepal, stretching from Dhaulagiri to Kanchenjunga. There is a guest house here if you want to make an overnight halt. Daman also boasts a Nepalese government horticultural farm.

The road continues to the Palung Valley at 2300 metres, an area famous for the cultivation of potatoes. All along this route you can see marginal land on the slopes being cultivated, a clear indicator of the population pressure in the hilly areas. The road passes through a serpentine series of curves, known as *seven turns* in Nepali, before descending to the tropical village of Dhunibesi at 750 metres. The valley is an important producer of guavas, mangoes and bananas and from the town of Naubise in this valley the road to Pokhara branches off. A steep 700-metre climb then takes you over the final hill before descending to Thankot, the first village in the Kathmandu Valley and only a short drive from the city.

If you want to fly from Birganj to Kathmandu you must first take the short bus ride to Simra, where the airport is located. RNAC makes two flights daily on this short sector. The fare is Rs 205 and the flight takes less than half an hour.

TO POKHARA FROM SUNAULI

The easiest way to get to Sunauli, at the Indo-Nepal border near Nautanwa, is to take a bus from Gorakhpur. The UP Roadways buses are slower and more

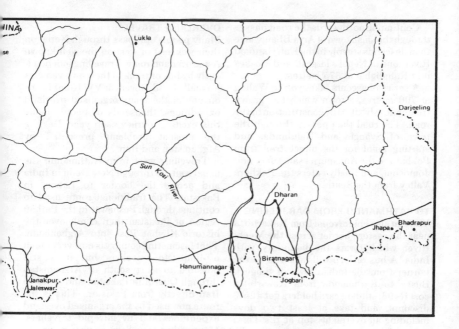

crowded. It is better to take a tourist bus at Gorakhpur (near the bus and railway station) and you can reach the border in less than three hours for Rs 13. There is also a railway service between Gorakhpur and Nautanwa near the border but it is slower and less frequent and, therefore, not recommended.

If you arrive late in the evening and would like to go to Kathmandu or Pokhara early in the morning, there is the *Ajay Vijay Lodge* and *Mamata Lodge* at Sunauli near the border. Doubles cost Rs 35 and a bed Rs 10. Both are very basic and may be OK if you just want to overnight. If you want to stay in a better place you have to go to Bhairawa, three km away – see the Terai section.

At 7, 9 and 11 am express buses leave Bhairawa for Pokhara and charge Rs 37. It is better to backtrack to Sunauli on the border where the buses start to make certain of getting a good seat. From the town of Butwal, a few km to the north,

buses leave almost every hour but they take longer to reach Pokhara as they operate a local service.

Like the road between Birganj and Kathmandu this road was constructed with Indian assistance and is about 200 km long. It is, however, a better road. It crosses the Terai to Butwal then climbs over the Siwalik and Mahabharat ranges. Two hours out you reach the beautiful town of Tansen, which at 1271 metres is pleasantly cool if you have just left the hot Indian plains. Around the bus terminal you can have a meal at one of the many good *bhattis*, hotels run by the local Thakalis. Nearby is the *Siddhartha Hotel*, if you wish to stop for the night. If you do stay then make sure of climbing the hill, known as Srinagar, to admire the Himalayan view stretching from Dhaulagiri to Manaslu. Tansen is a small town inhabited mainly by Newars. It used to be the most important town in west-central Nepal and was the regional administrative centre.

Continuing northwards the road passes through the small town of Arya Bhanjyange then descends steeply to the Kali Gandaki River, one of Nepal's largest, and crosses it at Ramdighat at 375 metres.

A series of ascents takes you to Waling at 700 metres, a town which has grown tremendously after the construction of the road. The road then passes through the town of Syangja and Naudanda, and starting point for the direct trail from Pokhara to the Annapurna sanctuary and Jomosom, and finally enters the Pokhara Valley from the South.

TO KATHMANDU FROM DARJEELING

You can also enter Nepal from Kakarbitta near the eastern border across the Mechi River which forms the boundary with India. A bus or jeep will take you to the border from the Indian town of Siliguri. Buses to Kathmandu from Kakarbitta cost Rs 98, student card holders get a 25% discount, and take at least two days including an overnight stop at the Terai town of Janakpur. Until you meet the Birganj to Kathmandu road this route runs through the Terai just a few km south of the Siwalik Hills. Dense forest and new settlements are visible north of the road and the bus also passes through Biratnagar, a major industrial area and the centre of the jute industry. Later you will see the beautiful foothill town of Dharan and cross the barrages of the mighty Kosi River which causes much damage by flooding. The road as far as Janakpur was constructed under Indian assistance and from there to the intersection north of Birganj was constructed by the Russians. This route is often impossible in the monsoon as there are few bridges built yet. It is possible to fly from Bhadrapur, only a short bus ride from Kakarbitta, to Kathmandu on Mondays and Fridays for Rs 760. Sometimes the Bhadrapur-Kathmandu flight may be cancelled. But there is always a flight between Biratnagar and Kathmandu.

OVERLAND TRAVEL

Many people still pass through Nepal on their way east or west on the well-known Asian overland route. Travelling independently by bus or train, in their own vehicles – usually Land-Rovers or VW Kombis – or on one of the many organised overland expeditions, thousands of people make this exciting journey each year. Despite the present problems presented by Afghanistan and Iran.

Travelling west from Kathmandu the usual route is through New Delhi in India and across the border to Lahore in Pakistan. The traditional route used to continue through Peshawar in the Pathan region of Pakistan then climb over the historic Khyber Pass into Afghanistan. That fascinating country is now very much off-limits to travellers but it is still possible to skirt south of Afghanistan through Quetta in Pakistan and cross to Iran directly from Pakistan. This is the route now used by the organised overland expeditions and by intrepid travellers. Many other travellers, however, simply leap right over the trouble zone by flying from India or Pakistan to the Gulf or to other centres in the Middle East like Amman in Jordan. The traditional route, on the other hand, continues across Iran and into Turkey. There is a choice of routes across Turkey but most people pass through Erzurum and the capital Ankara before finally leaving Asia at the Bosphorus crossing in Istanbul.

Travelling east from Nepal most travellers fly to Bangkok, often with a week's stop-off in Burma, then travel down through Thailand and Malaysia to Singapore. Frequent flights and a weekly ship link Singapore with Jakarta, the capital of Indonesia. There are several routes across Java through Yogyakarta and on to the magical island of Bali. More adventurous travellers can 'island hop' south from Bali to Australia or cross over to Sumatra from Penang in Malaysia and travel the length of that wild Indonesian island before reaching Jakarta. Details of travel in both

Top: Shiva and Parvati look out from their temple in Kathmandu
Left: Nepalese house beside the path to Swayambunath
Right: Wood carving on Basantapur Durbar in Kathmandu

Top: Peacock window in Bhaktapur
Left: Temple strut at Changunarayan
Right: Bodhnath stupa

directions from Nepal can be found in *West Asia on a Shoestring* and *South-East Asia on a Shoestring* both published by Lonely Planet Publications.

A number of companies operate expeditions from Kathmandu to London and vice versa over a variety of routes and at a wide range of costs. Average time from Kathmandu to London is 70 to 90 days but there are shorter and longer trips.

Onwards to Tibet

It is now possible to travel to Tibet from Nepal. An agreement signed between China and Nepal in March 1985 allows travellers to enter Tibet along some specific points along the Sino-Nepalese border, including Kodari. It may also be possible to trek around Everest in Nepal and in Tibet, the same as for circum-navigating Annapurna in Nepal. In the near future there will be air services between Kathmandu and Lhasa if the flow of tourists warrant it.

ENTERING NEPAL BY AIR

Kathmandu is off-line for all the international airlines. Most air travellers from Europe will fly up from Delhi by Royal Nepal Airlines or Indian Airlines. Travellers from North America or Australasia generally enter from Bangkok by Thai International, Burma Airways Corporation or Royal Nepal Airlines. It is also possible to fly to Kathmandu from Hong Kong via Royal Nepal Airlines; or from Rangoon in Burma; Dhaka in Bangladesh, Singapore, dubai, Karachi; or Calcutta, Varanasi and Patna in India.

Airfares in early 1985 were:

Bangkok	– US$284
Hong Kong	– US$506
Delhi	– US$142
Calcutta	– US$ 96
Patna	– US$ 41
Varanasi	– US$ 71
Colombo	– US$460
Dhaka	– US$ 92
Rangoon	– US$239
Singapore	– US$285
Karachi	– US$226
Dubai	– US$444

There is a cheaper IT Excursion fare available in many of these sectors.

Flying from Bangkok it is possible to include, at no extra cost, a seven-day stopover in Burma. Visas for Burma can be obtained in Bangkok or Kathmandu. International Student Card holders under 26 years of age are allowed a 25% reduction on external and internal flights on Royal Nepal Airlines. A similar discount in given to under 30-year-olds in Indian Airlines. There is also a 25% discount available from Indian Airlines to under 30-year-olds, even if they are not students, if the fare is paid in convertible currency. Foreign residents of India and Nepal (those employed in missions, volunteers, etc) can get a 25% discount on a round trip fare between Kathmandu on the one hand and Delhi, Calcutta and Varanasi on the other. However, the trip must be completed in two weeks. If a cheaper excursion fare is used, no other discount (i.e. student) is available.

Travelling between Kathmandu and Delhi the budget conscious traveller can more than halve costs by flying Indian Airlines to Patna and then continuing by train to Delhi in less than 24 hours. Total costs by this method will be less than US$40. Curiously the cost of a Kathmandu-Patna and a Patna-Delhi ticket is also less than a direct Kathmandu-Delhi flight. By travelling this way, a saving of US$10 can be made. It is possible to make Patna-Delhi reservations for the same day's flight from Kathmandu.

The flight into Nepal will give you a superb view of the mountains in clear weather – if you choose the correct side of the aircraft. Flying from the east – Bangkok, Rangoon or Calcutta – try to be on the right side of the aircraft. If you are flying from the west – New Delhi or Varanasi – then try to be on the left side of the aircraft. Kathmandu's International airport is named Tribhuvan Airport after the late king. It used to rejoice in the name Gaucher – cow pasture – field!

ENTRY AND EXIT

Nepali customs are fairly lax on entry but quite systematic on departure to ensure visitors do not export antique works of art or marijuana. The usual, rarely enforced, regulations apply to how much of what you're allowed to bring into the country. The only requirement it might be advisable to worry about is the per person limit of twelve rolls of film. If you intend being considerably over these limits it may be wise to check with the Nepalese embassy before departure.

On departure there is a Rs 100 airport tax; domestic flights are also subjected to a Rs 10 airport tax if the ticket is paid for in Nepalese rupees instead of in a convertible currency. The airport has a duty free shop selling the usual range of cigarettes and liquor which must be paid for in US dollars. The experienced shoestring traveller will no doubt be familiar with the considerably greater value of these items in other Asian countries. A carton of 555 cigarettes and a bottle of Johnny Walker Red Label is a very advisable investment if Burma is your next stop.

Approximate costs and times for rail travel, 2nd to 1st class, between major Indian cities and the rail heads for Nepal are:

For Kathmandu

Calcutta-Muzaffarpur (train)	15 hours	Rs 70 to Rs 200
Muzaffarpur-Raxaul (bus)	3 hours	

For Kathmandu & Pokhara

New Delhi-Agra (train)	3 hours	Rs 100 to Rs 300
Agra-Varanasi (train)	13 hours	
Varanasi-Sunauli (bus)	9 hours	

If you are planning to tour India after Nepal, Indian Airlines offers a worthwhile excursion fare. Fourteen days unlimited travel on domestic services can be obtained for US$375. Indian Airlines domestic flights are, however, very heavily booked and to make best use of this opportunity it is wise to plan your itinerary carefully and make reservations well ahead. Indian Airlines also offer a 25% discount to people under thirty years of age but fares must be paid in for convertible currency.

ARRIVING IN KATHMANDU

After arriving at Kathmandu one should sit on the steps of the temples of Durbar Square and just watch people walking and buying.
Andre Christoph, France

If you arrive in Kathmandu by air you will find the hotel reservation counter as soon as you depart from customs and immigration. Only the more expensive and heavily booked hotels take reservations here, if you're heading for a cheap hotel you will have to front up and ask. Outside you'll be immediately surrounded by people claiming to be agents for the hotels and lodges – usually the cheap ones. If you go to the hotel they have in mind for you they may even offer a free ride. If you are paying look for a metered taxi – the ride into town should not cost more than Rs 25 at the most and by a direct route with a good meter could be less than Rs 20! Make sure the meter is turned on and working!! Now metered taxis add 10% to the fare recorded on the meter. There are also unmetered taxis which cost Rs 30-40. Royal Nepal Airlines offer a bus service into town for Rs 7 per person. The Royal Nepal Airlines office is at the top of New Road, the main shopping street in Kathmandu, only a short walk from the town centre. If you are on a budget, and don't have much luggage, you might also take the local bus from the airport to Ratna Park for only Rs 1.

Arriving by road from the Indian border or from Pokhara the bus will take you almost to the centre of town at the foot of the Bhimsen Tower near the post office.

This is only three blocks from the town centre, some of the minibus services will run you right into the centre. By whatever means you get into town, taxis or bicycle rickshaws around town are very cheap, a rickshaw ride should rarely cost more than Rs 5.

The best way to visit Kathmandu is to wander without aim, then you see everything – by getting lost you discover the most.

Gilles Callet, France

Getting Around

FLYING

Royal Nepal Airlines operate a number of scheduled and charter flights around the country. Aircraft used are Avro 748s on the major routes and short take-off and landing – STOL – Twin Otters and Pilatus Porters to the smaller places mainly for trekkers. These trekking flights are not scheduled but during the season departures are frequent and tickets can be obtained from the trekking agents. It is advisable to book flights (domestic) seven to 10 days in advance.

Regular Destinations

Central Nepal: Baglung, Bhairawa, Bharatpur, Gorkha, Janakpur, Jomosom, Pokhara, Rumjatar, Simra

Western Nepal: Dang, Dhanagadi, Jumla, Nepalganj, Rukumkot, Sanfe Bagar, Silgarhi Doti, Surkhet

Eastern Nepal: Bhadrapur, Biratnagar, Lamidanda, Rajbiraj, Taplejung, Tumlingtar

Charter Destinations The following are the main destinations for trekking flights, remember you are only allowed 10 kg of baggage on these small aircraft. It may be possible to charter helicopters although RNAC does not do it any longer. However, it is still possible to charter Twin Otter and Pilatus Porter aircraft through RNAC to such destinations as Jomosom, Lukla and Manang.

Lukla or Shyangboche: 45 and 50 minutes flight from Kathmandu, in the Solu Khumbu region on the route to Everest.
Langtang: 25 minutes north of Kathmandu.
Dhorpatan: 90 minutes west in the Dhaulagiri mountain range area.
Jumla: 120 minutes east on the route to Rara Lake.
Jomosom: 60 minutes flight east towards the Annapurnas.

GUIDED TOURS

Travel agencies in Kathmandu organise scheduled conducted tours and private tours by car or coach to places of touristic interest. If your stay in Nepal is too short to permit exploration on your own, then it is best to join a conducted or private tour.

Everest Travel conducts a Rs 70 tour to the Durbar Squares of the three cities of Kathmandu Valley each Monday and Thursday morning. A conducted tour to Nagarkot on Monday, Wednesday and Friday to watch the sunset and sunrise over the world's highest peaks cost Rs 70 per person not including overnight accommodation. On Wednesday and Sunday afternoons they run conducted tours to the temples of Pashupatinath, Bodhnath and Bhaktapur for Rs 60.

Kathmandu Travel has conducted tours to Pashupatinath, Bodhnath and Bhaktapur on Monday, Thursday and Friday mornings for Rs 70. Tours to Kathmandu City, Swayambhunath and Patan on Monday, Wednesday, Thursday and Friday afternoons cost Rs 70. On Tuesday and Sunday mornings there is a Rs 125 tour to watch the sunrise on Everest from Nagarkot.

These agencies and others such as *Yeti Travels* and *Gorkha Travel* will also arrange private tours if requested, at widely differing prices. Most agencies will arrange tours to Budhanilkantha to see the sleeping Vishnu. *Kathmandu*, *Gorkha* and *Shankar Travel* all arrange tours to the temple of Changunarayan. Almost all agencies organise a trip to Dhulikhel along the road to the Chinese border and to the border itself. Some agencies, like *Kathmandu Travel* for Rs 60, organise conducted tours to the temple of Daxinkali to watch the animal sacrifices on Tuesday and Saturday mornings. Occasionally overland bus companies will use their vehicles for tours during the periods between their trips.

DO-IT-YOURSELF TRANSPORT
Cars can be hired through *Gorkha Travels* (tel 2-14895) or American Express (tel 2-13596) in Kathmandu. The cost is fairly high both in terms of initial hiring charge and fuel – over US$3.50 per gallon. Full day charges are about US$30-40 including petrol and the services of a chauffeur. It is no longer possible for the clients to rent 'drive yourself' cars. Taxis, on the other hand, are quite reasonably priced – any ride around town should come to less than Rs 20 and a taxi can be hired all day for Rs 200 to 300. Taxis add a percentage to the meter reading because of fuel price increases. A group of people can tour the valley quite cheaply by taxi. A number of garages, particularly around Freak St, hire out motorcycles by the day or week but at about Rs 300 per day they are quite expensive. Recently, metered auto-rickshaws have become quite common in Kathmandu and cost as little as half of what you would pay for a cab.

Bicycle rickshaws only cost Rs 3 to 5 for any ride around town but be certain to agree a price before you start. For the fit and healthy bicycle hire is the ideal way to get around – the valley is sufficiently compact and flat to make riding a pleasure. Daily hire charges vary from Rs 7 to 10; get up early for the best selection of bikes and make sure you lock you bicycle when leaving it. Check the brakes before taking it out!

To discover the Kathmandu Valley with its three cities there is no better way than by bicycle, it costs less than Rs 5 a day and they can be hired in different places around the city.

Joelle Lambelle, France

but

If you do not like bicycles the bus service is inexpensive and well organised but during the monsoon enquire about the condition of the roads.

Genette Katz & Nadine Cals, France

PUBLIC TRANSPORT
Bus travel around Kathmandu and the valley is very cheap although often equally crowded. Less sardine-like but also inexpensive are the smaller mini-buses and the curious little three-wheeler tempos. The three main bus stations are all situated around the parade ground.

Post Office and Martyr's Gate: Buses and tempos to Patan

Bhimsen Tower near the Post Office: Buses to Pokhara and the Indian border

Bagh Bazaar, near the Park and Clock Tower: Buses east the Bhaktapur

City Hall: Buses to Pokhara, Janakpur and the Indian border Dhuliklel and points along the road to the Chinese border, Jakarbitta (eastern border of Nepal near Darjeeling)

Opposite the park near the clock tower: Buses to Bodhnath, Kirtipur, Pashupatinath, Patan and the airport.

Balaju, Lazimpat and Maharajgunj Tempos leave from the same National Theatre location for these three places and charge Rs 1.25. Many of the embassies are located in the Maharajgunj area.

Patan Buses leave along the park near the clock tower, they depart every 15 minutes and charge 85 paisa. Tempos depart from the Post Office as soon as they have six passengers. The ride costs Rs 1.25 and takes 10 minutes.

Bhaktapur Buses leave every 20 minutes between 6 am and 8 pm from the stop near the Clock Tower. The mini-buses charge Rs 1.25. You can also get to Bhaktapur by the new trolleybus service which runs from the statue at Tirprusewar through Thimi to the outskirts of Bhaktapur for 50 paisa. It is a 15 minute walk from the trolleybus terminal to the city centre in Bhaktapur.

Budhanilkantha Buses to the Sleeping Vishnu leave from the National Theatre near the lake and charge Rs 1.25 or you can travel by tempo for Rs 2.

Daxinkali Buses to the temple of Daxinkali where animal sacrifices are performed, leave from near the park and the Clock Tower on Tuesday and Saturday mornings. A cheap way of doing it is to take a bus to Pharping from the Martyr's Gate in the morning and get off at the boarding school near the temple.

Dhulikhel & along the Chinese border road to Lamosangu Buses to these places leave from the big bus terminal near the City Hall. There are departures almost every hour for Dhulikhel or Banepa and the fare to Dhulikhel is Rs 4.50. Buses to Barabise or Lamosangu out towards the Chinese border depart at 6 am, 10 am and 2 pm.

Pokhara Buses leave in the early morning near the Post Office or at the big bus park near the City Hall. It is advisable to reserve seats and buy tickets at least a day in advance.

Indian Border Buses to Birganj and Raxaul or Janakpur and the eastern border near Darjeeling can be found at the City Hall bus park.

Bodhnath Mini-buses charge Rs 1 to Bodhnath and leave from in front of the Park Restaurant, they depart when full. Pashupatinath is an intermediate point and the name of the stop is Gosala.

Kirtipur & the University Buses charge Rs 1 and leave every 15 minutes from the Park Restaurant, there are also mini-buses.

Godavari To go to the botanical garden take a bus to Lagankhel and change.

Trisuli To reach this starting point for the Langtang trek go the the main dairy at Lainchaur near the British Embassy. Walk three blocks west on the road leading in that direction until you reach the bus station known as Sorakutte Pati, buses also leave here for Kakani. It costs Rs 16 for Trisuli.

Swayambhu (Monkey Temple) Although there are no buses to the temple from Kathmandu city centre, there are taxis which can be shared for Rs 2. Taxis leave from Bangemudha (halfway between New Rd and Thamel) and head for the bottom of the hill where Swayambhu Temple is located.

Around the Valley

KATHMANDU VALLEY

If you arrive by air the Kathmandu Valley will be the first place you visit in Nepal. As far as art and architecture are concerned your visit to Nepal need go no further than the valley. Three important cities in the valley, the most important being Kathmandu itself. Patan, the most 'Buddhist' of the three is across the Bagmati River to the south of Kathmandu, but so close as to be almost an extension of the capital. It is known to this day for its excellent works of art and carvings in wood and bronze. Bhaktapur, also known as Bhadgaon, is the most 'mediaeval' of the lot and is situated in the eastern part of the valley. While Kathmandu and Patan have undergone great changes in the two decades since Nepal ended its long isolation, Bhaktapur has changed very little and is still much as it was three decades ago; some would say three centuries. In the early eighties, the German-aided project in Bhaktapur helped to make it cleaner and provided such amenities as private latrines in most of the homes.

Kathmandu stands at about 1350 metres and the valley is surrounded by hills of an altitude around 2400 metres. The original inhabitants of the valley were a people known as the *Newars* and they still form a majority of the population. Typical Newar towns in the valley are Thimi, Bode, Chapagaon – south of Patan and Sankhu. There has also been much migration from other parts of the country, mainly by Brahmins and Chetris who can be found in suburban areas of Kathmandu and Patan, and in villages to the western side of the valley. Many of the people living in the hills surrounding the valley are Tamangs.

Until Nepal's unification process from small principalities and kingdoms started two hundred years ago, there were small independent kingdoms in the valley. The kingdoms of Kathmandu, Bhaktapur and Patan all had amazingly sophisticated art and architecture, especially during the 17th century which was the golden age for the construction of temples and palaces in the three cities. It makes a romantic picture to think of these three mediaeval kingdoms nestled in a fertile valley in the Himalayas – sometimes fighting each other, but more often celebrating numerous feasts and festivals, and competing in the building of temples and other works of art. In the same era temples and idols were being indiscriminately destroyed in India. The affluence of the valley was assured by its strategic position on a major trade route between Tibet and the north Indian plains. The kings of the valley were sometimes Hindu and sometimes Buddhist.

Then in 1768 King Prithvi Narayan Shah started his campaign to unify Nepal. The three kings of the valley were defeated and the foundations of a united Nepal were laid. The use of the Nepali language, one of the Indo-European family of languages, replaced the Tibeto-Burmese Newari language of the valley as the language of administration.

Today the valley is the most developed part of Nepal with a network of roads and electricity in most of the villages. The availability of improved seeds, fertilisers and extensive irrigation has allowed the farmer to cultivate wheat as well as the traditional rice. Two decades ago rice was often the only crop. Land reform programmes have allowed the farmer a larger share of produce which once had to be given to the landlords.

KATHMANDU

Kathmandu is both the capital of Nepal and the largest city in the country. Most of the interesting things to see in Kathmandu are clustered around the old part of town between the old market place and the new

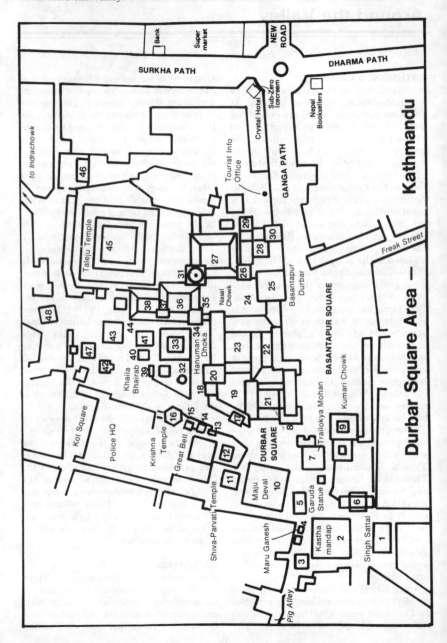

Kathmandu — Durbar Square Area

SURKHA PATH

NEW ROAD

DHARMA PATH

Bank

Super market

Crystal Hotel

Sub-Zero Icecream

GANGA PATH

Nepal Booksellers

to Indrachowk

Tourist Info Office

Freak Street

Taleju Temple

45

46

48

38 37 36 35

31

27

29
28 30
26
25
24

Basantapur Durbar

BASANTAPUR SQUARE

43
44
41
40
39
42
47

33

32

Khaila Bhairab

Hanuman Dhoka

34

23

22

Nasal Chowk

Kumari Chowk

Kot Square

Police HQ

Krishna Temple

Great Bell

16
15
14
13

18
20

19

21

9

Trailokya Mohan

7

8

DURBAR SQUARE

6

Maju Deval

10

11

12

5

Garuda Statue

Shiva-Parvati Temple

Maru Ganesh

Kastha mandap

2

Singh Sattal

1

3

4

Pig Alley

1	Sing Sattal Temple	25	Basantapur Durbar
2	Kastha Mandap	26	Bangla Tower
3	Shiva Temple	27	Mul Chowk
4	Maru Ganesh	28	Basantapur Chowk
5	Laxmi Narayan Mandir	29	Laxmi Bilas
6	Kabindrapur	30	Bilas Mandir
7	Trailokya Mohan	31	Panch Mukhi Hanuman
8	Gaddi Baithak	32	King Pratap's Column
9	Kumari Chowk	33	Jaganath Mandir
10	Maju Deval	34	Hanuman Statue
11	Vishnu Temple	35	Narsimha Statue
12	Shiva-Parvati Temple	36	Mohan Chowk
13	Great Bell	37	Mohan Chowk Tower
14	Stone Vishnu	38	Sundar Chowk
15	Saraswati Mandir	39	Khaila (black) Bhairab
16	Krishna Mandir	40	Indrapur
17	Bhagawati Mandir	41	Vishnu Mandir
18	Sweta (white) Bhairab	42	Kotilinggeshwar Mandir
19	Masan Chowk	43	Kakeshwar Mandir
20	Degutaleju Mandir	44	Stone Inscription
21	Hnuluche Chowk	45	Taleju Temple
22	Lam Chowk	46	Tana Deval
23	Dahk Chowk	47	Maha Vishnu Mandir
24	Nasal Chowk	48	Mahendreshwar Mandir

shopping area along New Road. Around the central Durbar Square are the old Royal Palace, a number of interesting pagoda and Indian style temples and the Kumari Devi, residence of the living goddess. Some of the interesting things to see in the Durbar Square area include:

Kalo Bhairab (39) This huge stone-image of the terrifying Black Bhairab was once used as a form of lie detector. Suspected wrongdoers were forced to touch the feet of the god and swear whether they had committed the crime. It was said that lying brought immediate death!

Sweta Bhairab (18) Hidden behind the lattice work on the temple wall behind Black Bhairab is the even more terrifying aspect of White Bhairab. This figure was built in 1794 by King Rana Bahadur Shah, the third king of the Shah dynasty, and it is used today as the symbol of Royal Nepal Airlines. The windows are opened for only

a few days each year to reveal the image during the Indrajatra festival in September. You can peer at him through the lattice.

Taleju Temple (45) This beautiful three-storey golden pagoda style temple was dedicated to the family deity of the Malla kings. It was built in the 16th century but unfortunately entry inside the temple is not allowed to foreigners.

Stone Inscription (44) Walking along the outside wall of the palace from the Taleju Temple towards the statue of Hanuman you come across a stone inscription written in eighteen languages, including English and French. It was set up by King Pratap Malla in the 17th century; he was both a poet and scholar. Legend says that milk flows from the spout in the middle of the inscription if somebody manages to read all the different languages.

Hanuman Dhoka The statue of the legendary figure from the Ramayana stands cloaked in red at the gate to the Royal Palace. His face has long been obscured by the red paste placed on it by faithful visitors. The figure is protected by an umbrella and flanked by two poles with the unique double triangle flag of Nepal. Entrance to the palace costs Rs 5.

I went for a walk down to the centre of Kathmandu during my first day. I felt as if I was going through a trip back in time, a pure fantasy. I did not judge, believe or disbelieve. I just looked at what seemed like an exhibition – a street panorama of mediaeval living. The only jolt to remind me of the present century was the odd car honking its way through the narrow streets. In fact, the sight of cows, goats and chickens going their way alongside the colourfully clad human inhabitants of this mediaeval town was bizarre to say the least.

Craig Bailey

Royal Palace The old Royal Palace takes its official name, Hanuman Dhoka Palace, from the figure at the entrance door – it translates as 'the palace with the statue of Hanuman at the gate'. The palace was originally built by King Pratap Malla in the 17th century but was renovated many times later as the Shah kings lived here till the end of the 19th century. There are many courtyards inside the palace. You can enter the most famous one, the **Nasal Chowk** (24), and climb to the top of the ancient nine-storey **Basantapur Tower** (25) that overlooks it.

As you enter you will see a very artistic and beautiful image of **Narsimha** (35) killing a demon with its nails. The picture gallery on the left contains portraits of the Shah kings and the seats used by the Malla kings. It was on the platform in the centre of this main courtyard that King Birendra was crowned in the 1975 coronation ceremony. A horse, which is believed to be a deity and which no one is allowed to ride, is sometimes walked around the platform.

UNESCO are renovating the four red coloured buildings around the courtyard and the tallest has been completed. These four buildings are supposed to represent the four ancient cities of the valley – Kathmandu, Bhaktapur, Patan and Kirtipur. They are the Bangla or **Kirtipur Tower** (26), the Laxmi Bilas or **Bhaktapur Tower** (29) and the Bilas Mandir or **Lalitpur (Patan) Tower** (30) as well as the dominant **Basantapur (Kathmandu) Tower** (25). The Malla kings were supposed to be born on the first floor of the Basantapur Tower and granted audiences on the second floor. With their queens they would watch dancing from the third floor. From the fourth floor the kings would look out over the town before meals, to ensure smoke was coming from every household – food was being cooked and no one was going hungry. The view from the very top looks down on New Road, Freak Street and Durbar Square today, and far over the valley. The courtyard next to the white building to the south-east has a small temple where Malla kings, whose bodies were not taken to the burning ghats on the Bagmati, were cremated. There is also a small museum inside the Palace which contains a collection of items connected with the life of King Tribhuvan (1906-1955), who played a very important role in bringing democracy to Nepal in 1951. You can also see the royal throne of Nepal and a numismatic museum.

King Pratap Malla (32) The statue of a king seated with folded hands, surrounded by four sons, and situated on top of a pillar facing the palace temple, is supposed to be this most famous Malla king.

Drums and Bell (13) The giant drums, across the road next to the police station, were built in the 18th century, as was the bell, which was erected sixty years after those of Patan and Bhaktapur. At that time any unique addition to one of the valley towns' Durbar Squares was immediately copied by the others!

Kumari Devi (9) The three-storied building with the artistic windows looking out on to Durbar Square, and its door guarded by stone icons, is the Kumari Devi – house of the living goddess. The continued veneration of a young girl, as if she were a living goddess, is part of the magic that makes Kathmandu a 'living museum'.

The big gate beside the Kumari Devi conceals the huge chariot which takes the Kumari around the city of Kathmandu once a year. Entering the house you reach a courtyard surrounded by balconies with 18th century masterpieces of woodcarving. Perhaps you might catch a glimpse of the goddess at the windows. She is a young girl and easily recognisable by the black shadowing around her eyes which extends as far as her ears, and by her hair which is piled up over her head. Photographing her is not allowed. The courtyard contains a miniature stupa with a symbol of Saraswatic, the goddess of learning, on its side, looking like a star of David, and a mandala on a lotus. Non-Hindu or Buddhist people are not allowed to go beyond this courtyard.

The Kumari is not born a goddess nor does she remain one all her life. She is usually chosen from a caste of Newar goldsmiths when she is about five years old. It is essential that she has never been hurt or shed blood. After careful screening by a number of people, including the astrologer, the selected candidates, about 10 in number, are locked in a dark room where fearful-looking masks and freshly slaughtered buffalo heads are kept. Frightening noises are made from outside and the girl who shows least fear is selected. She is installed on a throne in the room she lives in, during the Dasain festival. The spirit of the goddess is said to enter her body after this ceremony. As soon as she reaches puberty the Kumari becomes human once more and a new goddess must be chosen.

For three days each September during the festival of the God Indra – marking the end of the monsoon season – the Kumari is taken by chariot around Kathmandu. The Kumari also blesses the King of Nepal on this occasion, putting a red tika mark on his forehead and receiving a gold coin in return. It is said that the Kumari gave her blessing to the grandfather of the present King very reluctantly in the year that he died. People say that she was feeling very sleepy and had to be literally forced to mark his forehead. The Kumari goes out officially five to six times a year during the major festivals including the big and small Dasains in October and April when she appears at the old Royal Palace, Hanuman Dhoka.

The present Kumari was only five years old when she was selected. When she reaches puberty she will return to her parents' home only three blocks from the Kumari Devi. Her expenses are paid by revenue from *Guthi*, the lands under the ownership of temples or deities. These funds provide adequate amounts of rice, salt and dal but meat and firewood have to be purchased separately. The Kumari also gets a considerable sum in offerings from devotees. The Kumari is not supposed to go to school, but the last one has a visiting teacher and the present one is also being educated. When she retires she receives a government allowance of Rs 50 a month until she marries when a lump sum of Rs 1000 is paid as dowry. She gets no further allowance after marriage.

There is a popular belief that a man who marries an ex-Kumari may die within six months and should, therefore, be strong both physically and mentally. This could lead, not unexpectedly, to a general reluctance to marry a Kumari, but many people now believe this is simple superstition and cite cases of husbands outliving an ex-Kumari.

The institution of the Kumari dates back at least two centuries to the last Malla king of Kathmandu, Jayaprakash Malla. He once had intercourse with a prepubescent girl and as a result the young girl later died. The king was then told in his dreams to start the institution of the Kumari, worship her, and once every year

...And the wildest dreams of Kew
Are the facts in ——
Kathmandu

R. KIPLING ——

Dropouts, deadbeats
freaks, geeks
poseurs, mutants
& hangers out ——

THE SCENE IN DURBAR SQUARE

Hair tinted red, yellow and green

DAD TRYS HIS WINGS

USA XXX GRADE A FLOUR

....lounging on the temple steps

convey her around Kathmandu as penance for his sins. The institution may have existed even earlier and only the custom of the Kumari visiting the city by chariot started at this time. The last Malla king of Kathmandu was defeated on the day of the Kumari festival, and the first king of the present Shah dynasty received his blessing on that same day as was customary.

There are many other interesting sights to see around the Durbar Square apart from the continual bustle of Nepalese life itself. A pleasant hour can easily be spent sitting on the platform of the **Trailokya Mohan Temple** (7) or the **Maju Deval** (19) and watching the flute salesmen, trishaw riders, fruit and vegetable sellers, postcard hawkers and tourists below. The three-roofed **Trailokya Mohan** is easily identified as a temple to Vishnu by the fine Garuda kneeling before it. The large three-roofed **Maju Deval** with its nine-stage platform has some interesting erotic carvings and gives a good view over the square and out to Swayambhunath. From here you can look across to the **Shiva-Parvati Temple** (12) where images of the god and his goddess look out from the window on the activity below. The white neo-classical building looking highly out of place in the exotic Durbar Square is the **Gaddi Baithak** (8) which was built as a palace during the Rana period.

Erotic carvings There are several temples in the square with erotic carvings on the struts but the best carvings are those on the **Jagnath Temple** (33) beside the monkey god Hanuman. There are a number of explanations for the presence of these carvings on so many temples, but the most pleasing is that the goddess of lightning is a chaste virgin and would not consider striking a temple with such shocking goings-on.

At the top of Pie Alley, across from the Kasthamandap Temple is the small **Maru Ganesh** (4) temple dedicated to Ganesh and a constant hive of activity – Ganesh is

a very popular god. The **Shiva Temple** (3) slightly down from this is used by barbers who can usually be seen squatting on the platform around it. Many of the temples in the square were badly damaged in the 1934 earthquake and have subsequently been restored, rebuilt or modified. An excellent and highly-readable description of the history; significance and architecture of many of the Durbar Square building can be found in *An Introduction to Hanuman Dhoka* published by Tribhuvan University and available very cheaply in Kathmandu.

Kathmandu will provide many other interesting sights to the casual wanderer. Set out from the centre and explore the mazed alleys and crowded squares of the market area north of the Durbar Square. You'll find many surprises. The white, minaret-like **Bhimsen Tower** was constructed as a watch tower by a prime minister and is of no particular significance but serves as a useful landmark. It was renovated after suffering serious damage in the 1934 earthquake.

It is interesting to visit Mahakal Temple opposite the hospital in downtown Kathmandu. There is a legend that Mahakal, great death, enters this temple every Saturday. I felt a definite presence there one Saturday, a kind of excitement in the air as people streamed past the image. Perhaps it was the ancient God or maybe just the effect of so many people, bells, incense, etc. – go and find out some Saturday.

Richard Schifman, USA

Walking Tour of Old Kathmandu
The road from Kathmandu Durbar Square to Rani Pokhari (lake) is perhaps the most famous street in old Kathmandu. Although the New Road or Durbar Marg may signify new Kathmandu, there is no match for the above road on the number of different items that can be found in its colourful shops, activities taking place, as well as the number of temples and people that can be encountered along the road. The road, which was not paved until the '60s was actually the main road for Kathmandu before the Great Earthquake of 1934

flute vendor

many flower sellers in the courtyard cater principally for religious ceremonies. On the right-hand side, the wide road which leads to New Road is named in honour of a martyr who helped overthrow the Rana regime. The shops along this road sell electric and consumer goods imported from Hong Kong and Singapore. A large number of Indians visit Nepal to purchase these goods which are not readily available in India. A road heading to the left from Indrachowk leads to Thamel which has recently emerged as a centre for budget travellers in Kathmandu. In Indrachowk Square itself, as you turn to the right (after the wide road), you will see a narrow alley where bangles and beads are sold, popular with Nepalese women. Woollen rugs and hand-woven carpets are sold from a platform under the Shiva Temple.

Kel Tole, which contains the Temple of White Machendranath, is a place where traditional music is played and open to westerners. Watch for the interesting statue of Buddha on top of a pillar near the entrance to the temple. To the right are a number of stores which specialize in Nepalese caps.

Further on, the next square is called Asan, the busiest in Kathmandu, and has six roads radiating from it. The three-storey-high pagoda is that of the goddess Annapurna (goddess 'full of grain'), while the two-storey pagoda is dedicated to Ganesh. On the (western) left-hand side of the square are shops which sell dried fruit. The road heading to the north has sidewalk-based merchants selling fruit and vegetables.

Two roads lead from Asan to the fenced lake called Rani Pokhari. Just before you reach the lake, you will see a large building (facing west) which was called the 'Durbar School' and was the oldest school in Nepal to teach English. It was founded in the 19th century. It is now named after Bhanubhakta, the Nepalese poet.

which occured just before the construction of the New Road.

Start from tour from Durbar Square (see the description) in front of the high Pagoda (the Taleju Temple). Walking to the east, the courtyard on the left is called 'Kot' where a great massacre took place in 1846 and was the start of the Rana regime which lasted a 100 years. Further on, again on the left is a replica of a small temple of Pashupatinath. This contains a copy of the idol in the famous Pashupatinath Temple, prohibited to all non-Hindus. You can see the five headed idol, a Shiva image, from the outside. This locality, called Makhan Tole, Nepali for 'butter', and is known for the many shops which sell Tanka painting and clothes.

Continuing along, the next square reached is called Indrachowk, the 'court-yard of Indra', named after an ancient Hindu deity. On the left of the square the building with the metal lions peering from the windows is the Temple of Akash Bhairab (the Bhairab of the sky). The

PATAN

Patan – sometimes called Lalitpur, the

city of beauty – is Kathmandu's near neighbour, the second biggest city in the valley and the most Buddhist. Patan can be easily reached from Kathmandu by bicycle, bus or tempo. Buses and tempos stop at the large **Gate to the City of Patan** from where it's a 10 to 15-minute walk along narrow alleys to Durbar Square.

In the last few years a very large number of small handicraft shops have opened in Patan and it is an ideal place to buy fine bronzes and woodwork at reasonable prices.

Patan reminds me of Venice because of its red brick, the peaceful surroundings and the serenity of its people. But most of all, it reminds me of the beauty of Nepal.

Erberto Lo Bue, Italy

Hiranya Varna Mahabihar Walking from the bus stop, shortly after passing the cinema and before the road turns right, a sign to the left points to one of the most beautiful Buddhist monasteries in Nepal. The monastery, built in the 12th century, takes its name from the gold-plated roof which was dedicated by a rich merchant. Patan once had many such families who became quite affluent from their Tibetan trading. Inside the monastery there are many prayer wheels and scenes from the life of Buddha on the walls. The courtyard has a richly decorated three-storeyed temple with an image of Buddha; this monastery is quite unlike anything else in Nepal.

Kumbeshwar This five-storeyed temple to Shiva can be found further down beyond the Hiranya Varna Mahabihar. The water in the courtyard spring is said to come directly from the holy lake in Gosainkunda.

Durbar Square Another five minute walk brings you to the Durbar Square where the ancient royal palace of Patan is located. The British writer Landon had this to say of the square at the beginning of this century:

As an ensemble, the Durbar Square of Patan probably remains the most picturesque collection of buildings that has been set in so small a place by the piety and pride of oriental man.

Most of the buildings in the square were built in the 17th century by the famous Malla king of Patan, Siddhinarsingh Malla. The Royal Palace and Taleju Temple stand on the left side of the square while the temple of Krishna and a host of other temples stand on the right. Patan's biggest market place, the Mangal Bazaar, is also around the square.

Bhimsen Temple The first temple on the right can be discerned by the pillar in front with a lion on top. Bhimsen was a figure from the epic Mahabharata and according to the legend one of the strongest men who ever lived. The three-storeyed temple has a golden-coloured facade on the first floor.

Shiva Temple The second temple with two stone elephants guarding the door is that of Shiva. Shiva's animal, the bull, is on the other side of the temple. The first floor is quite artistic and there are erotic carvings on the roof support struts.

Krishna Mandir The third temple, dedicated to Krishna, is the most famous in the Durbar Square. Built by King Siddhinarsingh Malla in the 17th century it was influenced by Indian architecture, not the usual pagoda styles. The mythical manbird Garuda sits with folded hands on top of a pillar since Krishna is the incarnation of Vishnu and the Garuda was his animal. The stone carvings at the top of the first-floor pillars tell the story of the Mahabharata while the second floor carved scenes are from the Ramayana. A major festival is held here in August on the occasion of Krishna's birthday. A characteristic feature of this temple is that there are no nails or wood and the construction is entirely of stone.

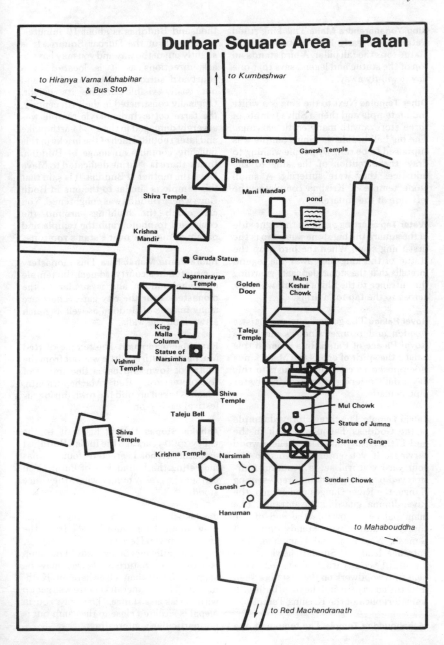

Durbar Square Area — Patan

to Hiranya Varna Mahabihar
& Bus Stop

to Kumbeshwar

Ganesh Temple

Bhimsen Temple

Shiva Temple

Mani Mandap

pond

Krishna Mandir

Garuda Statue

Jagannarayan Temple

Golden Door

Mani Keshar Chowk

King Malla Column

Statue of Narsimha

Taleju Temple

Vishnu Temple

Shiva Temple

Mul Chowk

Statue of Jumna

Statue of Ganga

Taleju Bell

Shiva Temple

Krishna Temple

Narsimah

Sundari Chowk

Ganesh

Hanuman

to Mahabouddha

to Red Machendranath

King Yoganarendra Malla This king ruled Patan in the early 18th century and his statue tops the tall pillar. A bird stands on top of the statue and legend says that one day it will fly away.

Other Temples Next to the king is a white Indian temple and then a Shiva temple of three storeys with many erotic carvings. The big bell beside the Shiva temple was supposed to be rung by people wishing to draw the attention of the king to the injustices they were suffering. A small stone temple of Krishna completes the left side of the square.

Water Tap Starting again on the right side of the square the big stone water tap is the first thing seen. When the bird atop the statue of the king flies away the legend foretells that the stone elephants guarding the entrance to the Shiva temple will walk across to the tap for a drink.

Royal Palace The golden gate and artistic wooden and bronze windows mark the Royal Palace of Patan. In a room in this palace the spirit of one of the Malla kings is supposed to continue to exist; to this day a daily offering of tobacco in a water pipe is made.

Taleju Temple The three-storeyed temple of the Goddess Taleju was built in the mid-17th century and has excellent wood carvings. If you enter and go into the courtyard you will see a beautiful four-storeyed pagoda with statues representing Ganga, the River Ganges and Jumna, the River Jumna, guarding the entrance. The main palace is towards the end of the courtyard and outside stands statues of Ganesh, Narsimha and Hanuman. The entrance leads to Sundarichowk or the 'beautiful courtyard'. There is very beautiful woodwork on the first floor seen from the courtyard and the royal bath with a small replica of the Krishna Temple.

Mahabouddha Temple The temple of one thousand Buddhas is about 10 minutes' walk south of the Durbar Square. It is slightly out of the way and you may have to ask directions as it is located in a courtyard surrounded by buildings and not easily visible despite its height. Originally constructed in the 14th century, the terra cotta, Indian-style temple was severely damaged in the 1934 earthquake and later rebuilt. Each of the bricks in this building contains an image of Buddha. Inside there is a shrine dedicated to Maya Devi, the mother of Buddha. It is said that this temple is similar to the one in Bodh Gaya where Buddha was enlightened. You can climb the buildings around the courtyard to photograph the temple and obtain a fine view over Patan's rooftops.

Rudra Varna Mahabihara This monastery is situated in a courtyard near the temple of Mahabouddha and is similar to the monastery near the city gate. There are many images of Buddha as well as much artwork on the walls.

Rato Machendranath The temple of Red Machendranath is a little way out from the centre of town and has a fine image of Avalokitesvara, Red Machendranath, which is taken around the town during his festival each year.

Ashoka Stupas During his visit to the valley 2500 years ago the Indian Buddhist emperor Ashoka erected four stupas indicating the boundaries of Patan. You can see the grassy humps where they once stood.

Jawlakhel The Tibetan refugee camp is only about 10 minutes' walk from the centre of town. Here you can see carpets, rugs and pullovers being made. The camp is closed on Saturday. Prices may be slightly lower than elsewhere in Kathmandu. The handicrafts centre was set up with Swiss assistance. The only zoo in Nepal is situated close to the camp but is not particularly interesting.

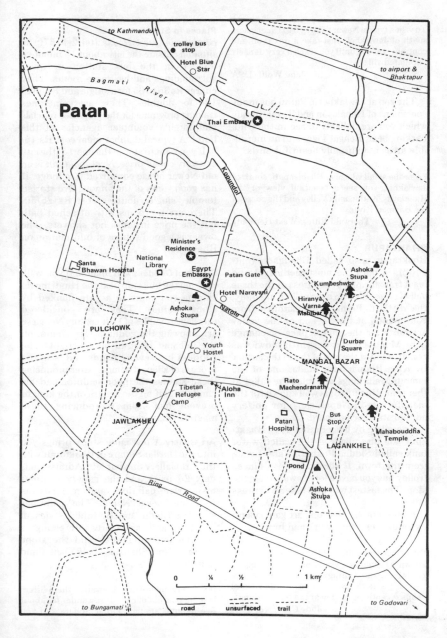

Patan

to Kathmandu

trolley bus
stop
Hotel Blue
Star

to airport &
Bhaktapur

Bagmati River

Thai Embassy

Kopundol

Minister's
Residence

National
Library

Santa
Bhawan Hospital

Egypt
Embasssy

Patan Gate

Ashoka
Stupa

Kumbeshwor

Hotel Narayani

Hiranya
Varna
Mahibar

Natole

Ashoka
Stupa

PULCHOWK

Durbar
Square

Youth
Hostel

MANGAL BAZAR

Rato
Machendranath

Zoo

Tibetan
Refugee
Camp

Aloha
Inn

Bus
Stop

JAWLAKHEL

Patan
Hospital

Mahabouddha
Temple

LAGANKHEL

pond

Ring Road

Ashoka
Stupa

0   ¼   ½   1 km

to Bungamati

road

unsurfaced

trail

to Godovari

To visit a typical Newar village go to Chapagaon, south of Jawlakhel. Just take a dirt road and continue walking until you reach a very densely populated village.

Jane Wolff, USA

The zoo at Jawlakhel in Patan has many specimens of Himalayan and Terai wildlife which you are unlikely to see in the wild: barking bear, Bengal Tiger and an incredible array of unusually beautiful birds.

From the small village of Bhainsepati, south of Jawlakhel, you see a beautiful view of the Himalayas, Kathmandu Valley and the gorge of the Bagmati River.

Thorwald Ritter, West Germany

BHAKTAPUR

Bhaktapur, also called Bhadgaon (bat-gown), is both the most mediaeval and least transformed by progress of the three valley cities. It's also been called, unkindly, the dirtiest. Perhaps its distance from Kathmandu at the far end of the valley accounts for the slower pace of change here. Much of the art work in this town was constructed at the end of the 17th century by King Bhupatindra Malla, one of the famous Malla kings who ruled the valley at that time. Bhaktapur is well known for the manufacture of Nepali caps, for pottery and for its delicious curd.

Travelling by bus or minibus to Bhaktapur you disembark at the walled water tank called Siddha Pokhari, a short walk from the town. If you travel by Chinese trolley bus you have a longer walk from the stop. The fastest way is to take an express bus.

Bhaktapur also has one art gallery and two museum – woodwork and bronze.

One of the specialities of Bhaktapur is its curd known as Jujudhau which means the king of curds in Newari. During autumn and winter it is perfectly safe to taste it in one of the several shops recently opened near the bus station.

Judy Crawford, USA

Places to Stay/Eat

Bhaktapur Guest House (tel 2-11670) is situated outside the city about 15 minutes' walk from the bus station in quiet surroundings and has large rooms. They charge Rs 35 to 65 for a single and Rs 55 to 100 for doubles. There are sometimes training programs for the Nepalese officials and foreign volunteer agencies at this hotel. A typical dalbhat meal cost Rs 15.

If you want to stay in the heart of the city at a very cheap price, *Nyatapola Inn* is an old Newar house converted to a lodge. It has good views of the famous five storied temple. singles/doubles cost Rs 25/50. There are no rooms with attached bath but the price includes hot showers. The owner is a good source of information on Bhaktapur.

Statue of Goddess and Bhairab If you walk up from the bus stop past the Hindi movie cinema you come to a gate flanked by stone statues. They are considered excellent examples of 17th-century Nepalese art, showing the goddess Ugrachandi on the left and Bhairab on the right. The goddess has several hands and is in the process of killing a demon. After producing these statues the poor sculptor had his hands cut off on the orders of the king to prevent him from reproducing these magnificent works.

Art Gallery A few more steps brings you into the Durbar Square of Bhaktapur with the Art Gallery on your left. Admission is only 20 paisa and the gallery contains many rare paintings and manuscripts from mediaeval Nepal. The paintings showing Hindu and Buddhist styles of Tantrism are particularly interesting as are the fine miniatures and the stone figure of Hari Shankar – half Vishnu and half Shiva.

It is very interesting to watch the potters making pots out of clay. Just wander for about five minutes around Durbar Square and you will come across several potters making different kinds of utensils and pots.

Heinz Aulenbach, Austria

Golden Gate Adjoining the gallery is the Golden Gate of Bhaktapur built by the last Malla king in the middle of the 18th century. According to Percy Brown, who visited Nepal in 1912, this was the liveliest work of art in the whole of Nepal. A Garuda, the vehicle of Vishnu, tops the gate and is shown eating serpents, its traditional enemies. The other, multi-headed figure riding the Garuda is the goddess Kali.

Statue of King Bhupatindra King Bhupatindra Malla, one of the most famous of the Malla kings, was responsible for much of the buildings and works of art in Bhaktapur in the late 17th century. His image sits with folded hands on the top of the pillar facing the gate. This representation of the king on a pillar, and a similar one in Patan, was copied from the one in Kathmandu's Durbar Square.

Fifty-Five Windowed Palace On the other side of the gate stands the palace which was first constructed in the 15th century and renovated in the late 17th. Opposite the palace is a large bell known as the *barking bell*. King Bhupatindra set it up in the late 17th century to avoid the effects of a bad dream, even today people say that dogs bark and weep when the bell is rung. The Durbar Square also contains a replica of the Pashupatinath Temple, built in the 15th century, with some athletic erotic carvings on the struts.

Kathmandu busker

Nyatapola Temple The five-storeyed Nyatapola Temple is both the highest temple in the valley and one of the finest example of Nepalese architecture and craftsmanship. The temple is visible from the Durbar Square and only a short walk away. King Bhupatindra constructed this temple at the beginning of the 18th century and is said to have laid the foundations himself, after which the temple was built in just a few months. The stairway leading to the temple is flanked by two wrestlers, then two elephants, two lions, two griffins and finally two goddesses. Each pair is supposed to be 10 times more powerful than the preceding one and even the wrestlers at the bottom are 10 times as strong as any mortal man. One of the

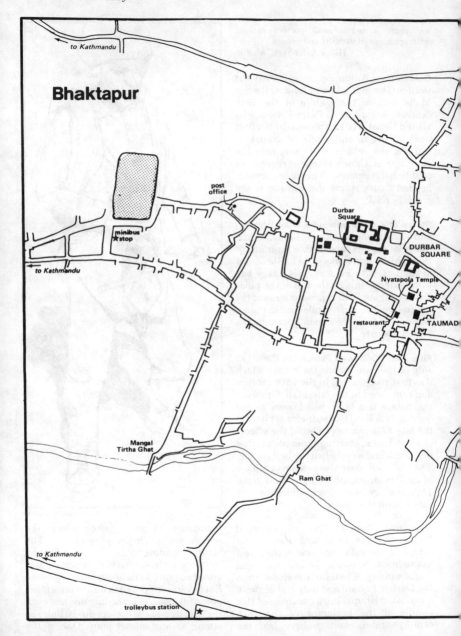

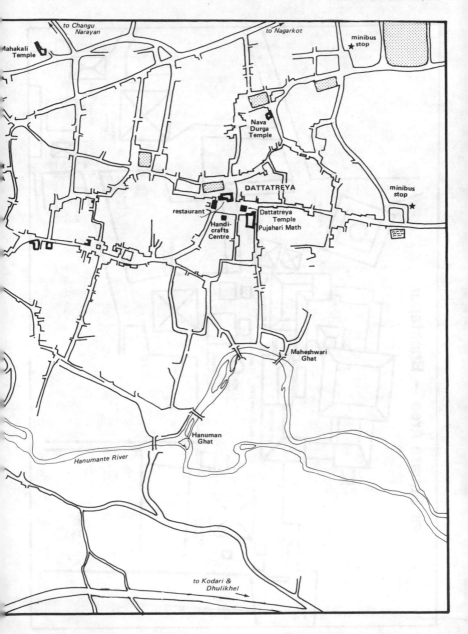

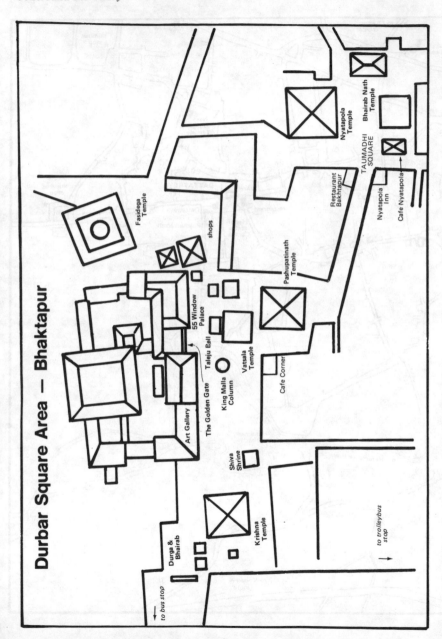

Durbar Square Area — Bhaktapur

to bus stop

Durga & Bhairab

Krishna Temple

Art Gallery

The Golden Gate

Taleju Bell

King Malla Column

Shiva Shrine

Vatsala Temple

Cafe Corner

55 Window Palace

shops

Fasidega Temple

Pashupatinath Temple

Restaurant Bakhtapur

Nyatapola Temple

TAUMADHI SQUARE

Bhairab Nath Temple

Nyatapola Inn

Cafe Nyatapola

to trolleybus stop

finest views of the temple can be had from
the road running out of the valley towards
the Chinese border. The whole town of
Bhaktapur can be seen backed by the
mountains and with the five storeys of the
temple rising majestically over the lesser
buildings.

In Bhaktapur there is a new restaurant, built
like a traditional Nepalese temple, right in the
square with the Nyatapola Temple. Excellent
views from the restaurant balcony but the food
is not so special.

Maureen Wheeler, Australia

Bhairabnath Temple The two-storeyed
Bhairabnath Temple stands on the right
of the Nyatapola and was originally
constructed early in the 17th century. It
has been rebuilt after suffering severe
damage in the 1934 earthquake and is
unusual for having a rectangular base.

Dattatraya Temple Only five minutes' walk
from the temple of Nyatapola brings you
to the square containing the Dattatraya
Temple and the Pujahari Math monastery.
Built in the 15th century this is the oldest
temple in the area and was dedicated to
Vishnu; as a Garuda-topped pillar and his
traditional weapons indicate. The temple
is said to have been constructed from the
wood of a single tree.

Pujahari Math The nearby monastery is
equally old and originally served as an inn
for pilgrims on the occasion of Sivaratri. A
chief monk still lives there. The wooden
carvings inside the courtyard are extraordinarily rich but the famous *peacock
window*, probably the finest carved window
in the valley, should definitely not be
missed. The window is in the small alley
alongside the monastery, on the left,
facing the main entrance. The restoration
work on the monastery was completed
with assistance from West Germany.
Further restoration work and the provision
of drinking water and sewage facilities to
part of Bhaktapur under the Bhaktapur

Development Project is also being assisted
by West Germany.

If you want to see another side of Nepal away
from the tourists and the comforts of Kathmandu, travel out to Thimi for a day to observe
Newari culture. It's not always easy to confront,
and not a place to go if you prefer the ease and
familiarity of westernized surroundings; but
you will be rewarded by a fascinating insight
into the daily life of the local people, as yet
relatively untouched by western influence.
Look out particularly for the beautiful pottery
made here.

Gillian, Andrew & Peter, UK.

SWAYAMBHUNATH
The Buddhist temple of Swayambhunath,
situated on the top of a hill west of the city,
is one of the most popular attractions in
Nepal. You can either take a taxi to get
there or walk in just 20 minutes from
Durbar Square. From the square a useful
shortcut is to go down Pig Alley, where the
pie shops are located until you reach the
river. Cross by the footbridge and keep on
going until you reach the base of the hill,
walking up to Swayambhu reminds me
somewhat of the Sacre Coeur in Paris. It is
one of the eight sights in Nepal included in
UNESCO's World Heritage List.

The stairs leading to the temple from
the east are quite steep and you might

prefer the gradual climb from the southern part of the hill where the restaurants are located. The temple has also been called the *Monkey Temple* as there are numerous monkeys roving around the place which thrive on offerings made by the devotees. They will entertain you by sliding down the handrail as you climb the steps. Be careful of them and do not carry any packages as they may snatch them from you.

The ever watchful eye of Buddha on the central stupa, the countless prayer wheels and the huge thunderbolt (Bajra in Sanskrit or Dorje in Tibetan) at the top of the stairs have long impressed visitors. Beside the stupa there is a large image of Buddha while the pagoda-style temple on the north-west side of the stupa contains a beautiful image of the goddess Hariti. She was the goddess of smallpox and used to devour children until Buddha made her stay near him and give up this bad habit. The complex also contains two Indian style temples, giving the visitor a chance to view a wide variety of architectural types. Swayambhunath gives a panoramic view over Kathmandu, particularly striking in the evening when the city is illuminated.

If you are lucky enough to be in Nepal during a full moon, try to spend part of it right up at Swayambhunath. Be sure to wander round the rear of the main stupa. There are many white stupas that glow peacefully under a full moon.

John Vogt, USA

Swayambhunath's stupa is reputed to be the oldest in Nepal. Although the earliest written reference to the place was made in the 13th century, there is little doubt that the site is very old – perhaps as much as 2000 years. Geologists now accept that the Kathmandu Valley was at one time a lake and according to legend this hill was then an island. Later in the 14th century, invaders from the south broke open the stupa to search it for gold.

When the horns of taxi cabs and music in the cold drink bars becomes too much, a short walk across the suspension bridge to the green hillside of Swayambhu will quickly relax you. Smile at the monkeys and see what happens.

Jonathan Hill, USA

Spend an afternoon, or a whole day, at Swayambhu, the monkey temple. It is a good bike ride from Kathmandu and then a steep climb up to the temple which is the centre of a tiny little village as well as a cluster of beautiful shrines. When you come down you can get good rice, dal and tea at the small roadside cafe at the foot of the hill.

Ara Jolly, England

A Warning Don't leave bikes near the shops on the way up unless you're prepared to pay protection money – otherwise they deflate your tyres. They own the only pumps for two km.

KIRTIPUR
Situated on a ridge to the south-west of Kathmandu, the mediaeval town of Kirtipur is interesting and attractive to visit. To get there by public transport you should take

a bus to the university and stroll up the hill to the ridge where the town is located. Kirtipur is a centre for cloth weaving, and dyed yarn hangs from many upstairs windows, while the clatter of looms can be heard from inside. The ridge also offers a fine view back over Kathmandu with the Himalayas rising behind.

When Kathmandu was being conquered by King Prithvi Narayan Shah of Gorkha, about two centuries ago, he met stiff resistance at this strategic point in the valley. Only after suffering heavy losses of men and materials was the king, who went on to unify all of Nepal, able to subdue Kirtipur. In order to avenge the deaths of so many of his soldiers the king cut off the nose of every able bodied man in the town. It is said that to this day the citizens of Kirtipur have noses that are shorter on average than anywhere else in the valley.

The campus of the university was named after King Tribhuvan, grandfather of the present king, and may also be worth a visit. The university library has the best facilities to be found in Nepal.

BALAJU

In the last decade the site of this beautiful park was just a village but seems now to be growing into a town and even merging with Kathmandu. You can get there by tempo from the National Theatre or walk in less than an hour as it is situated close to the northern outskirts of Kathmandu. The industrial district around Balaju is the most important in the valley but it does not affect the quiet surroundings of the park in any way.

Admission to the park costs just 20 paisa and inside there are beautiful bamboos and other trees, ponds with fish and the twenty-two gushing water-spouts that gave the park its name, 'Bais dhara Balaju'. There is also a modern swimming pool where you can enjoy swimming in the summer and a smaller image of the sleeping Vishnu at Budhanilkantha.

In front of the sleeping Vishnu a small, typically Nepalese, temple is flanked by a

row of Hindu images including elephant-headed Ganesh, Buddha protected by the hood of a serpent, and Bhagawati. A stupa-like structure shelters a many-armed goddess, unusual in a Buddhist stupa and an image of Harihar – half Vishnu and half Shiva. The hands on one side hold *trisul* a symbol of Shiva, while on the other side the hands hold *chakra* and *sankah*, the symbols of Vishnu. There is also a small phallic-shaped lingam surrounded by four pillars and an image of the bullock Nandi. The site is not more than three centuries old but makes an interesting visit due to this curious juxtaposition of Hindu deities.

PASHUPATINATH

Pashupatinath is the most famous temple in Nepal and is located on the route to Bodhnath. Although non-Hindus are not allowed inside the temple you can cross the river and view the temple from the hill on the other side. Near the entrance you will see many people selling flowers, incense and other offerings to be made to the deity. Inside is the golden pagoda and on the river banks you can sometimes see dead bodies being cremated on platforms. The Bagmati is a holy river like the Ganges and, like Varanasi in India, there is a burning ghat.

Pashupati, Lord of the Animals, is supposed to represent Shiva and the black image inside the temple has four heads. The temple itself is about three centuries old. It was renovated when the previous structures became decrepit. The idol is 600 years old, an earlier one was broken by Moslem invaders in the 14th century.

The big bull, Shiva's animal, inside the temple was built in the last century. The small bull in front of the temple is about three centuries old. Last year I visited the temple with a minister of the French government. He was so overcome by the site of it, he said: 'there are places like this where the spirit moves.' Some people are also reminded of Lourdes in France.

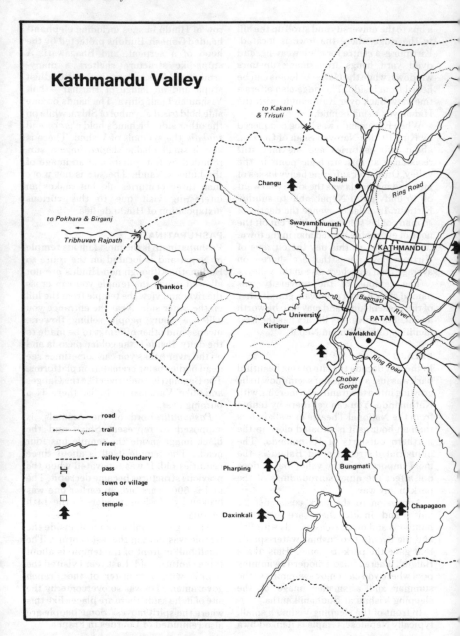

Kathmandu Valley

to Kakani
& Trisuli

Balaju

Changu

Ring Road

Swayambhunath

KATHMANDU

to Pokhara & Birganj

Tribhuvan Rajpath

Thankot

Bagmati
River

PATAN

University

Kirtipur

Jawlakhel

Ring Road

Chobar
Gorge

road
trail
river
valley boundary
pass
town or village
stupa
temple

Pharping

Bungmati

Daxinkali

Chapagaon

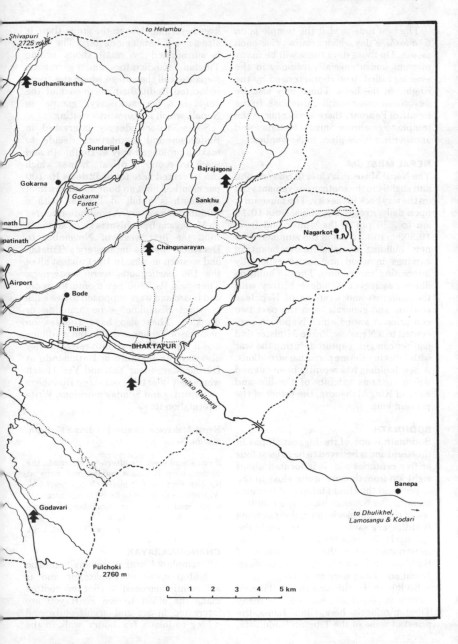

Shivapuri
2725 m

to Helambu

Budhanilkantha

Sundarijal

Gokarna

Gokarna
Forest

...nath

...patinath

Airport

Bajrajagoni

Sankhu

Nagarkot

Changunarayan

Bode

Thimi

BHAKTAPUR

Arniko Rajmarg

Godavari

Banepa

to Dhulikhel,
Lamosangu & Kodari

Pulchoki
2760 m

0 1 2 3 4 5 km

The best time to visit the temple is on *Ekadashi*, a day which occurs twice each month. On those days there will be many pilgrims and a special ceremony in the evening called *Arati* characterised by the ringing of the bells. There may also be devotional music and illuminations. In the month of February there is a big fair at the temple to celebrate Shiva's birthday and another fair takes place in November.

NEPAL MUSEUM

The Nepal Museum is close to Swayambhu and slightly to the south, a convenient visit on the way back to the city. The museum is open daily, except Tuesdays, from 10.15 am to 3.30 pm in the winter and from 10.30 am to 4.30 pm in the summer. The new building contains many beautiful carvings in wood and some especially interesting bronze idols. The old building illustrates recent Nepalese history with the uniforms and weapons of Nepalese soldiers and generals from the past two centuries. A sword which Napoleon presented to a Nepalese Prime Minister and leather cannons captured during the war with Tibet in 1856 are particular attractions. A new building has recently been opened which contains exhibits of the life and work of King Mahendra, the father of the present king.

BODHNATH

Bodhnath is one of the biggest stupas in the world and is believed to be at least four or five centuries old. It is located about eight km from the city, quite close to the airport and the Hindu temple of Pashupatinath. The bones of Kashyapa Buddha, one of the Buddhas who preceded Gautama Buddha, are said to be contained in the stupa. It is possible this stupa was constructed after the introduction of Buddhism in Tibet when relations between Nepal and Tibet were amicable.

Bodhnath is the centre of Tibetan culture in Nepal and you will see many Tibetan refugees here. Chini Lama, the priest of some of the Tibetan Buddhists,

lives here, and close to the stupa there is also a new Tibetan monastery. The stupa is surrounded by small shops selling Tibetan handicrafts and garments. Nepalese call the village where the stupa is located Bodh. Just north-east of the stupa is a big monastery, 'gompa' in Nepali, which is also worth visiting.

Some visitors, deeply interested in Buddhism and meditation, decide to make a prolonged stay at Bodhnath and there are rooms in private homes which can be rented here for as little as Rs 100 per month. About an hour's walk north of Bodhnath is a hill at Kappan with a Buddhist monastery. A meditation course on Mahayana Buddhism is given annually from the first week of November to December by the monastery's Tibetan and western monks. In 1981 almost all of the 150 participants were westerners. They paid Rs 1800 per month for room and board and were supposed to live a life of strict discipline – no smoking or drinking. They also have courses on painting of Tankas and Tibetan medicine and it is possible to go into retreat. They also have an Institute in Kathmandu at Durbar Marg (near Yak and Yeti Hotel) where they offer free courses on Buddhism on Saturday and Sunday mornings. Write information to:

Nepal Mahayana Centre PO Box 817 Kathmandu, Nepal

If you spend even one afternoon talking to the western-born Buddhist monks and nuns at Kappan monastery it might change your life. Western students can be found living there year round and rooms are available to those seriously intending to learn.

George Churinoff, USA

CHANGUNARAYAN

The temple of Changunarayan situated on a hilltop north of Bhaktapur and is sufficiently inaccessible that few visitors make the effort to see it. If you are interested in art and architecture and willing to take a few hours' walk in the

countryside then you will find a trip to this place very worthwhile. Changunarayan has several masterpieces of 5th and 12th century Nepalese art as well as the oldest stone inscription in the valley.

It is possible to combine a walking visit to the temple with a trip to the stupa of Bodhnath or the town of Bhaktapur. It is also possible to walk to Changunarayan after watching the sunrise from Nagarkot. The descent to the temple takes about four hours.

To reach Changunarayan from Bhakt-apur takes about two hours on foot. The hill, looking rather like Swayambhu, is visible to the north of Bhaktapur from the bus stop but it is best not to walk directly towards it as the trail is poor. For a better trail walk to the Durbar Square then follow any road heading north. A 10-minute walk through narrow alleys will take you to the northern edge of town where you can see the hill clearly. Simply follow the trail until you reach the bottom

of the hill from where it is a 15-minute steep climb to the top.

The pagoda style temple is dedicated to Narayana or Vishnu. The temple itself is not very old, perhaps two centuries, but the site is at least 15 centuries old. A Garuda, the mythical man-bird mount of Vishnu, stands in front of the temple with folded hands. It is supposed to have been set up in the 5th century and is one of the most important attractions in the valley. In front of the statue is the oldest stone inscription in the valley made in Gupta script and dating back to the same century.

The temple is flanked by four pillars topped by the traditional weapons of Vishnu including the lotus and conch. There are a number of images of Vishnu around the courtyard holding these weapons in his four hands. In the north-east corner of the courtyard there is an image of Vishnu riding a Garuda, this image is reproduced on the Nepalese Rs 10 note.

The site also contains an image of Vishnu superimposed on top of another image, one of the most picturesque and famous idols in the valley. It is supposed to date back to the 5th or 6th century although half of it is broken. There are a number of other outstanding statues from the 12th and 13th centuries including an image of Narsimha near the entrance. In Sanskrit the Narsimha means 'man and lion' and is supposed to be one of the 10 incarnations of Vishnu, in this case half-human and half-lion. The statue shows Narsimha killing a demon.

There is an interesting legend of how this incarnation took place – a demon pleased Brahma and in return received a promise that he could not be killed by a man or an animal, day or night, nor by any weapon. Unfortunately the demon then started terrorising the inhabitants of the earth and Vishnu himself had to take this man-lion (neither man nor beast) incarnation and use his nails (which were not a weapon) to defeat the demon in the evening (which is neither day nor night).

After leaving Changunarayan it is a short, steep descent to the river which can be crossed easily by a temporary bridge during the dry season. Two hours walk – passing the Royal Game Reserve at Gokarna – will take you to the stupa at Bodhnath. If your time is limited you can take a taxi from Kathmandu via Bodhnath along the same road and return the same way.

BUDHANILKANTHA

The image of 'sleeping Vishnu' at Budhanilkantha is probably the largest reclining image of Vishnu in the world. To get there you can take a bus in the morning from near the National Theatre or alternatively you can travel by bus or tempo to Bansbari, the site of a shoe and leather factory set up with Chinese assistance. From there it is about an hour's walk. The energetic could walk all the way from downtown Kathmandu in a couple of hours or, best of all, ride by bicycle.

Vishnu, sleeping on a bed of snakes, is supposed to have been carved from stone in the 11th century. According to legend Vishnu sleeps continuously for four months of each year, falling asleep with the beginning of the monsoon and awakening when it is over. Each November thousands of pilgrims come here for a big fair on the day he is supposed to wake up. The name Budhanilkantha has nothing to do with Buddha.

Another legend tells of the discovery of the image. A farmer was tilling his field one day and was terrified to find blood coming from the ground at the spot where his plough struck something. An excavation revealed the beautiful image of sleeping Vishnu.

Prayers take place here every morning around 9 am but the kings of Nepal are never allowed to go near the image. Should the king, who is himself supposed to be an incarnation of Vishnu, gaze upon his own image, it is said that he would be cursed. A smaller replica of the image has, therefore, been constructed near the swimming pool at Balaju for the king to visit if he desires. There is also a school, built with British assistance near Budhanilkantha – it is expected to become the best school in Nepal.

Take a trip to Sheopuri – highest mountain peak of the Valley. It is situated in the northern part and you should first go to Budhanilkantha from where it is a three to four hour climb – a full day's trip. The scenery is best because of the over 3000 metre height.

Wolfgang Korn, West Germany

GOKARNA & SUNDARIJAL

A pleasant couple of hours' walk in the vicinity of the Bodhnath stupa will take you to the old Newar village of Gokarna, north of the Royal Game Reserve. From Bodhnath take the road towards the reserve and turn left on to a dirt road after 20 minutes. Another 20 minutes' walk will bring you to the beautiful three-storeyed temple of Shiva called Gokarneswar, Lord

Top: Looking down from the Bodhnath stupa
Left: A typical rural scene in the valley
Right: Turning the prayer wheels around the stupa

Top: A group of Tibetan women at Bodhnath
Left: An old man twirls his prayer wheel
Right: Shop-houses around the great circle at Bodhnath

of Gokarna. The courtyard has an incredible collection of stone statues of deities from Hindu mythology such as Narad, Surya the Sun God, Chandra the Moon God, Kamadeva the God of Love besides the more conventional images of Shiva and Vishnu. Although they are probably only about a century old I have never seen such a collection in one place in Nepal.

After visiting the temple you can walk up to the village which is inhabited entirely by Newars and is surrounded by the game reserve on three sides. Although the village is so close to Kathmandu the villagers are very poor and many do not even speak Nepali.

Further down the road are the waterfalls of Sundarijal at the edge of the valley; a pleasant bicycle ride down quiet roads.

The Royal Game Reserve at Gokarna is a nice place to relax and get away from the hassles of Kathmandu.

Heidi Bauer, USA

A new company, Safari Park, has recently begun organising tours to the Royal Game Reserve. Its office is located in Durbar Marg and a round trip to the park costs Rs 25. Another way of visiting the park is to buy an excursion ticket for Rs 99. This includes round trip transportation from your hotel, entrance to the park and a one hour elephant ride. Inside the park, it is interesting to watch birds, monkeys and deer. Above all, you can get a glimpse of what the natural landscape and wildlife in the valley must have looked like before human settlement. It is also a popular picnic spot for Kathmanduites.

DAXINKALI

The best known temple to the Goddess Kali, the terrifying, is located on the southern edge of the valley. To get there takes about 45 minutes by car passing the narrow Chobar gorge on the way, through which flows the Bagmati River. A travel agency tour (Everest Travels and Kathmandu Travels) costs Rs 50 or you can travel by bus for Rs 5 round trip. The best day to visit Daxinkali is Saturday when crowds of Nepalese journey there to sacrifice chickens and goats to the blood-thirsty goddess. Tuesday is another, quieter, sacrificial day.

The temple is at the bottom of a steep hill with a small stream flowing close by.

After their rapid despatch the animals are butchered in the stream and their carcasses will later be brought home for a feast. It is interesting that sacrifices are always made to goddesses and must always be made with young male animals.

The scene around the altar is one of great chaos, gore and festivity, a visit to Daxinkali recalls the ritual sacrifice of animals which I had only read about in books.

Jack Peters, USA

CHOBAR GORGE

According to legend, when the valley was a lake and Swayambhu an island, Manjushree, the God of Wisdom, struck the rock at Chobar with his sword and released the valley's water. With the water thousands of snakes are supposed to have been swept out of the valley – leaving behind the snake king Karkotak who still lives close to the gorge in a pond called Taudaha. The Chobar Gorge is conveniently visited en route to Daxinkali and the beautiful temple of Pharping can also be included on the trip.

Close to the spectacular gorge is the first cement factory in the valley; unfortunately the Kathmandu Valley has a distressing physical similarity to the Los Angeles basin and major industrialisation or a large growth in the number of motor vehicles could lead to a similar affliction – smog.

The best view both of the mountains and Kathmandu Valley within easy reach (by car) of Kathmandu is obtained by driving out to Nagarjun forest about 3 km north of Balaju in Kathmandu. On payment of Rs 7 you will be allowed to drive through the forest, eventually, after 17 km reaching the mountain top, which is surmounted by a Buddhist stupa. An excellent view to the north of all the snow peaks from Annapurna through Langtang is obtained while the entire Kathmandu Valley is laid at your feet to the south.

Teve & Chris Hogan, England

Excursions from the Valley

If you are in Kathmandu between September and June the mountain flight, with its breathtaking views of the Himalayas, is an experience definitely not to be missed – even at a cost of US$55. The flight, made in the early morning lasts about one hour, and the aircraft, a 44-seat pressurised Avro Hs 748, flies at an altitude of over 6000 metres. During the flight you can view eight of the 10 highest mountain peaks in the world from a distance of less than 20 km. The aircraft flies along the length of the mountain range in both directions giving passengers on both sides an equal opportunity to view the peaks. In addition you are allowed to admire the view, individually, from the flight deck. A 'mountain profile', to help you identify the peaks is handed out before departure and afterwards the flight passengers are given a certificate to show that they have been 'greeted' by Mount Everest. The flight is especially exciting during the excellent weather and extremely good visibility of late October and November. Royal Nepal Airlines organise the mountain flights.

NAGARKOT

From the vicinity of Kathmandu the best view of the Himalayas, including Everest, can be obtained from the village of Nagarkot. Situated on a ridge to the northeast of the valley Nagarkot offers a view stretching from Dhaulagiri in the west to Kanchenjunga in the east.

Several travel agencies offer tours to Nagarkot from Rs 120 but the impecunious can take a bus to Bhaktapur, walk the several km to the ridge in a few hours, overnight at Nagarkot, and return to Kathmandu for less than Rs 25. During the monsoon period from June to September it is usually cloudy and you will only rarely be rewarded with a glimpse of the mountains. On the other hand the trek to the top will almost always result in a clear view during the months from October to April.

To get to Nagarkot leave the bus stop in Bhaktapur and walk to the centre of town where the Durbar Square is located. Head east from here and ask for the route to Nagarkot. As soon as you leave the city follow the road which passes a Nepalese Army barracks. An hour out from Bhaktapur you reach the city water tank by a cluster of bamboo trees and you can take a shortcut which saves two hours' walk. Leave the main motorable road and take the trail to the right. Forty minutes walk brings you to a stream, then a steep climb through beautiful pine forests takes you back to the main road. By using the shortcut, you can walk from Bhaktapur to Nagarkot in four hours.

The road to Nagarkot wanders to the left of the river. A trekker would save time if, after one hour's walk from Bhaktapur, he would follow a pipe that is Bhaktapur's water supply straight to the dam then climb the hill and keep the power line in sight all the way.

Gary Ott, USA

Recently a bus service – it's slow and very crowded, so try to sit up front – has started from Bhaktapur to Nagarkot and buses are available every three hours between 8 am and 4 pm for Rs 3. The buses start from the city bus stations and not from the trolley bus station. It is still pleasant to take the four-hour walk all the way from Bhaktapur except in the summer and the monsoon.

Nagarkot is more like a resort town than a village and contains ten hotels called 'lodges', 'guest houses' or 'cottages'. They are in all price ranges and have varying facilities. Some face the entire Himalayan range so that you can view Everest and other peaks just after coming out of your room. In others, you have to walk from 10

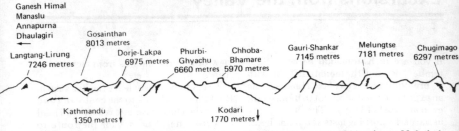

Ganesh Himal
Manaslu
Annapurna
Dhaulagiri

Gosainthan
8013 metres

Langtang-Lirung
7246 metres

Dorje-Lakpa
6975 metres

Phurbi-
Ghyachu
6660 metres

Chhoba-
Bhamare
5970 metres

Gauri-Shankar
7145 metres

Melungtse
7181 metres

Chugimago
6297 metres

Kathmandu
1350 metres

Kodari
1770 metres

to 25 minutes before reaching the ridge in order to view the peaks. As you need to walk very early in the morning to watch the sunrise in the Himalayas, it is essential that you stay close to the ridge unless you're driving. Not all the lodges have running water. Some provide good views of the Himalayan ranges but not of Everest.

The lodges are situated in clusters about two km apart along the ridge or at lower altitudes. It may be possible to bargain over the room prices, especially in the off season. The best location for a view of Everest is near the Nepal Army Barracks which is also the last stop of the bus from Bhaktapur. The hotels are situated in the following areas:

Southern Part of Ridge (near Army Barracks)
The lodge on top of the hill is *Taragaon-Nagarkot*, US$18 for a single with hot and cold running water, but a bit overpriced for what you get. *Nagarkot Guest House* on the eastern side of the ridge facing the Himalayan ranges, run by a Nepali woman named Didi, has good views but may be closed by 1986 because the lodge is on Army-owned land.

The two other lodges in the area, on the western side of the ridge, require a 10-minute climb to the road and the ridge. *Sun Rays and Moon Beams* is run by a Nepalese gentleman with a European wife. Doubles cost Rs 30 and dormitories cost Rs 10 per person. Both Nepali and western food is available. *Mount Everest Lodge*, nearby, has relatively cheap rooms.

Northern Part of the Ridge (near Mahakal Temple) There are two lodges in the area. *Nagarkot Lodge*, on top of the ridge, has good views and doubles at Rs 40-50. It's a 15-minute walk from the bus stop on the road to get there.

Lower Part of the ridge (west side) *Everest Cottage*, 50 metres below the ridge has rooms with attached bath. Singles/doubles cost Rs 66/88. There's also a big fireplace in the dinning hall.

On a clear day, it is worthwhile walking to the Tower on the ridge north of Nagarkot to get a better view of the peaks. It takes less than an hour and is an easy walk. It is interesting to trek for three to fours hours from Nagarkot (except during the summer or monsoon) on your way back to Kathmandu. There is also a cheese factory in Nagarkot and you can pick up a bit of lunch on your way back. While trekking back to Kathmandu, there are three possibilities:

Nagarkot-Sankhu-Bodhnath-Kathmandu
You can descend from Nagarkot to the valley in the north-west to the village of Sankhu, which is visible from there. The terrain, which is relatively easy, has not been walked much by western trekkers. Sankhu is a Newar town located in the middle of rich agricultural land. There are buses leaving for Kathmandu every hour and cost Rs 3. The ride takes about an hour and you pass the temple of Bodhnath and Gokarna Forest. You could also walk to Bodhnath from Sankhu in about two hours, instead of taking the bus.

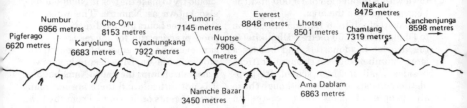

Pigferago
6620 metres

Numbur
6956 metres

Karyolung
6683 metres

Cho-Oyu
8153 metres

Gyachungkang
7922 metres

Pumori
7145 metres

Nuptse
7906
metres

Everest
8848 metres

Namche Bazar
3450 metres

Lhotse
8501 metres

Ama Dablam
6863 metres

Makalu
8475 metres

Chamlang
7319 metres

Kanchenjunga
8598 metres

Nagarkot-Changunarayan You can walk along the ridge from Nagarkot to the famous temple of Changunarayan in about three hours. This temple should not be missed by anyone interested in art and architecture (see the section on Changunarayan). On your way back to Kathmandu, you could descend either to Bhaktapur or to Bodhnath.

Nagarkot-Banepa You can descend to Banepa on the other side of Kathmandu. You start the trek near the tower at the southern part of the ridge and follow a steep descent to the valley in the east. On your way you will pass through the old Newar town of Nala. From Banepa, you can take a bus back to Kathmandu.

If you are overnighting in Nagarkot be certain to bring enough warm clothing as it can get very cold in winter or autumn. There is also camping space available. This trip, with its fine views of eight of the 10 highest mountain peaks in the world, is one the visitor to Kathmandu should not miss.

KAKANI
This village is situated on a ridge northwest of Kathmandu and offers good views of the western and central Himalayas. Although I personally prefer the view from Nagarkot those interested on enjoying the variety of Himalayan scenery, especially magnificent views of Ganesh Himal, should go there. It is quieter than Nagarkot but the food available has less variety and caters less to western tastes. To get there take a bus or mini-bus at Sorakhutte (five

minutes walk from Thamel) leaving from Trisuli (at 7 am and 1 pm). From there it is about one hour's walk along a dirt road to the top of the ridge.

DHULIKHEL & NAMOBUDDHA
Dhulikhel, a beautiful village just outside the Kathmandu Valley, gives a better view of the Himalayas than anywhere in the valley. In the late sixties the hippies, who had just started coming to Nepal in numbers, liked this quiet and sleepy Newar village so much that they decided to construct a temple right on the parade ground where you go to view the mountains. Although they were not permitted to do so you may think that their choice would not have been a bad one.

When you are in Dhulikhel, do not miss a visit to Panauti, you reach there after a pleasant two hour walk across ricefields along the course of a small stream. The beauty of this small town is due to its numerous temples and magnificent wood carvings.

Michel Thierry, France

Buses leave Kathmandu for Dhulikhel every hour and travel on the excellent road towards the Chinese border. While still in the valley you pass through Thimi, a typical Newar town which produces much of the vegetables for Kathmandu and also has a thriving cottage industry in pottery and mask manufacture. The road then skirts the edge of Bhaktapur and passes through a typical rural landscape of paddy fields at the eastern end of the valley. It winds over the Sanga Pass as it leaves the valley then descends to Banepa, a Newar town with a population of 10,000 and the biggest bazaar in the area.

A steep climb from Banepa brings you to Dhulikhel at 1500 metres. Dhulikhel is the district headquarters and boasts a large number of government offices besides a jail and high school. Its population consists of Newars, although there are people of many other castes in surrounding villages. Many tourists make early morning trips to Dhulikhel to see the awesome sunrise over the mountains. Travel agencies organise these trips from Rs 120. The budget conscious can travel there by bus and stay overnight for less than Rs 20. The best Himalayan view is obtained by climbing the small temple-topped hill to the east.

To see the sun coming up from behind the mighty Himalayas from the little temple up the hill from Dhulikhel is a thrilling sight, even worth getting up at 4 am.

Chris Whinett, England

The Dhulikhel Lodge (tel 114) has electricity and hot water and is one of the best cheap places to stay in Nepal. The manager, known as BP to his guests, has visited the US for a few months and is very receptive to western visitors and helpful with trekking information. The spartan rooms at the lodge costs Rs 20 per person. There are also dormitory beds and should the lodge be crowded you may have to be content with these – the lodge is particularly popular with volunteer workers. It is also a good place to meet other travellers. Nepali food, available at the lodge for Rs 10 also is popular.

A new *Hotel Dhulikhel Mountain Resort* (tel 4-11031) has opened four km away from Dhulikhel towards the Chinese border. The views of Himalayas are good but it is expensive as singles cost US$25 for bed and breakfast. The owner of Dhulikhel Lodge is constructing the more expensive *Sun and Snow Hotel* about a km away from Dhulikhel.

If possible while in Dhulikhel you should try to make the trek to Namobuddha, also known as Namura. The walk only takes three hours in each direction and is a good practice run for longer treks. This can even be an enjoyable trek in the monsoon season. BP will supply you with a diagram showing the trail to Namobuddha, it is not difficult and there are not many steep ascents or descents. From the town you pass to the south of the hill with the temple. Although there is a shorter route when returning it is advisable in the wet season as it may get very slippery.

The trek passes through interesting country and a number of small villages where you can ask for directions. The stupa at Namobuddha is relatively unknown and although it is probably not more than a few centuries old I have not been able to discover its exact age. There is an interesting legend behind the stupa at Namobuddha. One of the earlier Buddhas is said to have come across a tiger at the point of death and unable to find food for its cubs. The Buddha was so moved with compassion that he offered his own flesh to the hungry tiger. If you climb to the top of the hill from the stupa you reach the site where this event is supposed to have taken place. A carved stone tablet shows the Buddha offering his hands to the tiger. There is an interesting festival at this site in the month of November. You can trek back to Dhulikhel by an alternative route to avoid backtracking.

You can have some very good chang near the stupa at Namobuddha at a very cheap price.

Hans Wagner, West Germany

CHINESE BORDER

Only in Hong Kong is it as easy to get so close to China as you can by Nepal's 'road to the Chinese border'. There is not much to see there but it is nice to boast of having been to the border.

Most of Kathmandu's travel agencies operate tours to the border once or twice a week although it is wise to enquire if the road is blocked by landslides during the (which costs Rs 24 round trip) or getting a group together to go on an overland bus or truck.

You can take the mail car to the border or trek, the scenery as you walk is very nice. It is possible to buy tea in villages on the way and sleep on the floor. The road follows the river and there are many waterfalls. It is reasonably easy to hitch-hike along the road (alternatively bargain with lorry drivers) as it is a popular picnic spot.

Jay McLeary, Australia

The last stretch to the border is a dirt road running through a spectacular gorge. Shortly after the tarmac road ends there is a site where rice paper is produced. You can see the rice being ground down in a water-driven stone mill and the sheets of paper stretched out to dry in the sun. A few km south of the border at Tatopani, which means hot water in Nepali, there are hot springs if you fancy having a hot bath and watching China at the same time.

At Kodari, a bridge over the river separates Nepal from China. Sentries stand on both ends of the bridge and on the Chinese side there is a small barracks for soldiers. In the late 1960s a large portrait of Chairman Mao used to stand near the bridge on the Chinese side but it has since been removed. Nepalese traders and porters are permitted to cross the bridge and go into Tibet as far as the town of Khasa but it is not an open border as is the case with India.

No aspect of Nepalese foreign policy has been watched by the outside world with as much interest, concern and sometimes even alarm, as the decisions leading to the construction of this road. Nepal's viewpoint in this respect has not always been understood.

The highway has recently been renamed the Arniko Highway in memory of the renowned Nepalese architect who went to China during the 13th century. The highway starts at Bhaktapur in the Kathmandu Valley; apart from the recently

Buddha

monsoon. Kathmandu Travel and Tours (tel 2-14446) and Everest Travel (tel 2-12217) often have conducted bus tours to the border when the road is open. It is an all-day trip and cost about Rs 250.

Four times daily a bus service runs between Kathmandu and Barabise via Lamosangu – the starting point for the Everest trek. The first bus leaves at 6 am and the fare is Rs 16. On the way to the border you pass through the beautiful Panchkhal valley between Dhulikhel and Dolalghat, a well known area for the production of mangoes, guavas, sugar cane and rice. There are no buses beyond Barabise but you can get a ride on one of the many trucks going to the border for about Rs 5 or you can walk there in about five hours. There is a small lodge at Barabise where a single room costs Rs 6. Other ways of getting to the border include a ride on the early morning Post Office bus from Kathmandu to Dhulikhel

completed trolley bus system between Kathmandu and Bhaktapur the Chinese are also aiding the construction of another road between these two cities. The road leaves the valley through Sanga Pass and continues through Banepa, Dhulikhel, Panchkhal, Barabise and Tatopani, before reaching the Miteri Sanu or 'Friendship Bridge' at the Bhote Kosi River. A casual glance at the map will show that at this point a chunk of Chinese territory is also surrounded by Nepal and this is one of the narrowest points in the whole length of Nepal.

The highway generally follows the alignment of two rivers, an important characteristic of the Chinese constructed highways in Nepal as the Kathmandu to Pokhara road also follows the course of rivers. The length of the highway is 104 km and it includes one major bridge at Dolalghat. By car it takes about four hours to reach the border from Kathmandu. Kodari, the termination point of the highway, is at 1500 metres while the Tibetan town of Khasa, across the border, is somewhat higher at an elevation of 2200 metres. With the exception of Dhulikhel, few points along the road are noted for their views of the Himalayan range.

The lodge at Tatopani is peaceful and has a lovely setting. The proprietor and his family are hospitable and charming and serve good inexpensive food.

Andre Lelaid, Ken Przywaro, USA

The Chinese road has often been called the best highway in Nepal as there are few hairpin bends or steep sections. There are also comparatively few landslides during the monsoons. The bazaar towns along the route, such as Banepa, Dhulikhel and Barabise, are largely Newar but the hinterland is mainly inhabited by Brahmins and Chetris at lower altitudes and by Tamangs and Sherpas at the higher altitudes, particularly in the north.

The agreement for the construction of the road was signed in 1961 and the completed road was signed in 1961 and the completed road opened by King Mahendra in 1966. Much of the criticism the road has engendered has been about the threat it could pose to the security of Nepal and India. Nepal has maintained that the road is simply an expansion of a long established trade route and this opening up of a hitherto backward area was essential for its economic development.

Districts connected by the road have become much closer to Kathmandu and the first third of the road as far as Dhulikhel is heavily trafficked. Even as far as Dolalghat, the half-way point, the volume of traffic makes the road economically feasible. My own conclusions after visiting the villages along the road four years after its construction were:

'It could definitely be said that most of the villages in the area are better off today than they were four years ago. It is difficult to reach any conclusion regarding an increase in per capita income or agricultural production but there are now schools in almost every village and villagers now have the opportunity to be at least literate. The opportunity of getting education is not solely restricted to people belonging to higher castes; although caste rules continue to be followed there is a new flexibility in their observance. The number of early marriages has declined greatly but the practice of bigamy is still widespread despite preventive legislation. There is an increased tendency for the educated few of the villages to migrate to Kathmandu and settle there. Almost every village has a transistor radio and the villagers now have a chance to know what is happening in Nepal as well as in foreign countries.'

One of the largest magnesite deposits in Asia has been discovered a few km east of the road. If it were not for the road this deposit would never have been economically feasible. A road from Lamosangu to Jiri, built with a Swiss loan, passes through this deposit. The road has also made substantial indirect contributions to Nepal's economic development. Half the materials and machinery used in the construction of other Chinese-aided projects in Nepal – such as the Sun Kosi hydro-electric project producing 10,000 kw near Lamosangu or the Kathmandu-Pokhara highway – are estimated to have been brought along the road. Nevertheless the bordering region in Tibet is sparsely populated and economic activity is still low. It is also a long way from the populated and industrial areas of China. It is often cheaper to import materials from China by the sea route via Calcutta than directly along the road, but this will change as soon as there is more economic activity in the area.

Where to Stay

ORIENTATION

New Road is the most important road in Kathmandu and the city's shopping centre. It starts from the large gate near the Nepal Airlines office and ends at a statue of a Rana Prime Minister, several blocks west. The heart of New Road is around this statue. To the south is the headquarters of Nepal Bank – Nepal's largest. To the north is the supermarket which contains most of the recently opened stores selling electronic and consumer goods imported from Hong Kong and Singapore. The heart of old Kathmandu extends from Indrachowk to Asan further to the north. If you continue further west you enter the big Basantapur Square where the old Royal Palace is located. *Durbar* in Nepali means palace, and there are Durbar squares in Patan and Bhaktapur in front of each of their old palaces. But the King of Nepal no longer lives in the palace in the city centre and the royal palace was moved to Narayanhiti about a century ago on what was then the outskirts of the city. The Tourist Information Office is close to the New Road statue, just before you get to Basantapur Square. It can supply a large map of Kathmandu and other material about places to visit. There is also a dairy here where milk, cheese and other like products can be bought.

Freak Street Area

The road running off Basantapur Square to the south has, since 1973, rejoiced in the unofficial title of Freak Street. It used to be a wild jumble of cheap hotels, restaurants, hippies, money changers, hash smokers and all the freaky travellers of the road east. Like the equally well known Chicken Street in Kabul, Afghanistan, Freak Street is known to the travelling fraternity throughout the world. By the early eighties Freak Street had declined in popularity while the Thamel area in Kathmandu grew assumed greater favour. There are still, however, many cheap hotels and some cheap restaurants, and shops selling used trekking equipment. As it is quieter and less crowded than Thamel, some travellers still prefer it. One advantage of staying here is that you are very close to the heart of old Kathmandu whereas Thamel is about 20 minutes' walk away. You do, however, have to be a little careful of blackmarket currency and dope dealers. But hotels and restaurants are still the cheapest in Kathmandu and it is now much less touristy than Thamel.

Pie Alley (formerly Pig Alley)

A number of streets run out from Durbar Square; one of them, the unpaved road leading down towards the river from the Temple of Ganesh unofficially known as Pie (or Pig) Alley. As the name suggests it's not terribly clean, but it does contain some inexpensive hotels. Although the original area for pie shops, only two remain.

Kanti Path and Thamel Area

Starting again at the airline terminal end of New Road (near the city gate) a short walk to the right will bring you to the main post office, just under the foot of the Bhimsen Tower. Walking in the opposite direction will take you by the Government (Bir) Hospital, past an enclosed lake, the National Theatre, the German Embassy and the Yellow Pagoda Hotel before arriving at the new Royal Palace where the King of Nepal lives. The road continues into the embassy sector. Turning left at the Royal Palace a couple of blocks will bring you into the Thamel area which has recently emerged as a centre for low cost accommodation and restaurants (but not as low as Freak Street). Thamel is 15 to 20

74

minutes' walk from the centre of Kathmandu. It is amazing to see how this area has now become the 'centre' for budget travellers in recent years. This is perhaps due to the fact that the well-known Kathmandu Guest House is also in the area. Thamel, however, has become a very touristy area. There are indications that it is becoming more like Freak Street was in the late '70s.

The street running from the new Royal Palace to the Clock Tower is called Durbar Marg, and is a broad street containing most of the airline offices, travel agencies and several of the more prestigious hotels.

Patan (Jawlakhel) Area

For those who want to stay away from the Thamel, Freak Street or Pie Alley areas, a new tourist centre is now emerging near the zoo in the Jawlakhel district in Patan. This area also contains the only Youth Hostel in Nepal. Although the number of inexpensive lodges and restaurants in the area is quite small, the attractive thing about it is the easy access into Kathmandu via the many buses, tempos and minibuses. It is also near several embassies and aid agencies. The UN complex being built nearby is almost ready and all the UN agency offices are expected to move into the area before 1987. Many long-term foreign residents of Kathmandu like this area.

PLACES TO STAY

A great number and variety of hotels have opened in Kathmandu in the past five years. There remains a shortage of rooms in four and five star class hotels particularly during the October-November and March-April high seasons, but current building plans have almost erased this shortage. At the other end of the scale the impecunious traveller can easily find clean, comfortable decent places to stay for under US$3 a night including hot showers. Few cities in west or South-East Asia can offer such bargains.

Naturally the list of hotels that follows is by no means exhaustive, but it does include most of the hotels in each category which I assume would be found enjoyable by users of this book. Some hotels may add a 10% service charge to the prices quoted and all of them will charge 13-15% government tax. Don't be surprised if inflation has forced these prices up even though the categorization stays the same. Many of Nepal's hotels and lodges take their name from mountain peaks such as Annapurna, Makalu or Manaslu.

Places to Stay – top end
Soaltee Oberoi 5*

out-of-town location, tel 2-11211, 290 rooms, 18 suites, all with bath, aircon, four restaurants, two bars, shopping arcade, swimming pool, casino shuttle bus to city. Cable SOALTEE, KATHMANDU, telex 2203 SOALTEE NP

Hotel Yak & Yeti 5*

tel 4-11436, restaurants, bar, swimming pool, aircon, coffee shop, shopping arcade, close to city. Cable YAKNYETI, telex NP 2237 YKNYTI.

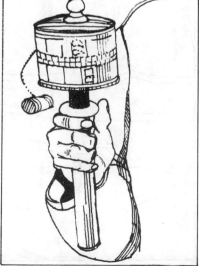

prayer wheel

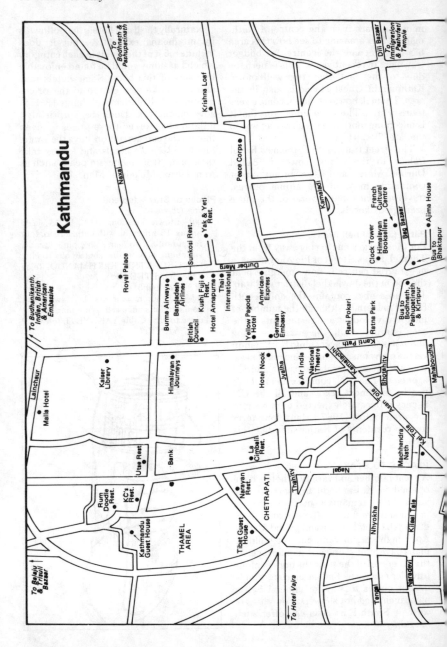

Kathmandu

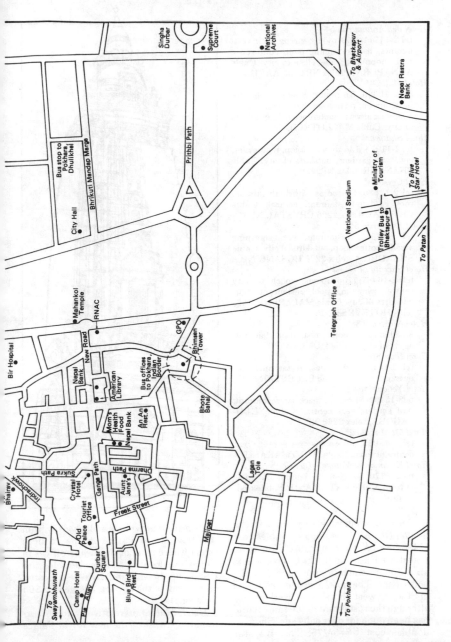

Hotel de l'Annapurna 5*
   tel 2-11711, 159 rooms, aircon, four restaurants, bar, swimming pool, conference
   hall, shopping arcade, close to city. Cable
   ANNAPURNA, telex NP 2205 AAPU.
Hotel Malla 4*
   tel 4-10320, 57 rooms, 8 suites, all with
   bath, aircon, restaurant, bar, tennis court,
   shopping arcade, conference hall, outskirts
   of city. Cable MALLOTELD.
Hotel Shankar4*
   tel 2-11973, 135 rooms, aircon, restaurant,
   lawn and gardens, outskirts of city. Cable
   SHANKER, telex NP2230.
Hotel Crystal3*
   tel 2-12630, 53 rooms with bath, aircon,
   roof garden, restaurant, central. Cable
   CRYSTAL, telex 2290 CRYSTAL NP.
Hotel Shangrila 3*
   tel 2-12345, restaurant, bar, shopping
   arcade, coffee shop, outskirts of city. Cable
   SHANGRILA, telex 2276 HOSANG NP.
Hotel Sheraton Everest
   tel 2-16467, 155 rooms, coach to city
   centre, swimming pool, restaurant, bar,
   outskirts of city. Cable MALARI NEPAL,
   telex HOTEVEST NP.
Hotel Narayani 3*
   tel-21711, 75 rooms, restaurant, bar outskirts of city. Cable HONARAYNI.
Hotel Blue Star3*
   tel 2-14135, 80 rooms, restaurant, bar,
   outskirts of city. Cable BLUESTAR.
Hotel Yellow Pagoda3*
   tel2-15492, 51 rooms, snack bar, restaurant,
   roof garden, very central. Cable YELO-
   PAGODA, telex 2268 NP.
Hotel Mt Makalu 2*
   tel 2-13955, 30 rooms, restaurant, bar,
   centre of town. Cable MONTMAKALU.
Hotel Kathmandu Village – Dwarika's
   tel 213770, 15 rooms, restaurant, outskirts
   of town. Cable KATHMANDAP, telex NP
   2239-KTP.

Kathmandu's oldest luxury hotel is the *Soaltee Oberoi* where singles/doubles cost US$64/82. A 10-minute taxi ride from downtown Kathmandu, the Oberoi boasts an outdoor swimming pool and Nepal's only casino. The *Hotel Yak and Yeti* is one of the newest hotels in Kathmandu although the restaurant of the same name has been open for over a decade. Singles/doubles cost US$55/75. The five star

Hotel de l'Annapurna is a block away from the New Royal Palace in the modern street where most of the airline offices in Nepal are located. Singles/doubles are US$55/68. *Hotel Sheraton Everest*, located on the way to the airport, charges US$65 for a single.

Hotel Malla, in relatively quiet sur-roundings west of the new Royal Palace near the Thamel area, charges US$40 for singles. The architecture is a mixture of Nepalese and western styles; the gate pillars are topped with lions, fish and peacocks similar to many Nepalese temples.

The *Hotel Shankar*, a short distance out of town in pleasant surroundings, charges US$35/45 for singles/doubles. This is the place to stay if you want to be close to numerous temples, the old Royal Palace and the Temple of the Living Goddess. It is clean and air conditioned, and offers fine views over the city from its upper terraces.

One of the nicest new hotels in the area where most of the embassies in Kathmandu are located, *Hotel Shangrila*, charges US$37/40 for singles/doubles. This is recommended. *Hotel Narayani* is actually situated in the city of Patan, just across the river from Kathmandu and is easily accessible. It charges US$30/39 for single/doubles. *Hotel Blue Star*, on the way to Patan from Kathmandu has rooms in a similar price range. *Hotel Yellow Pagoda* in Kantipath, near the new Royal Palace, Thamel and the city centre costs US$22/33. *Kathmandu Village Hotel – Dwarika's* is on the outskirts of town near the Temple of Pashupatinath. It has a collection of beautiful wood carvings on windows and is more like a quiet house in the countryside than a hotel. It won the Pacific Area Travel Association Heritage Award in 1980. Singles/doubles cost US$22/33. A very good place to stay if you do not mind the distance.

Places to Stay – mid-range

Hotel	tel	rooms
Ambassador	2-14432	35
Aloha Inn	5-22796	10
Paradise	2-12746	10
Nook	2-13627	20
Vajra	2-14545	38
Tibet Guest House	2-14383	31
Panorama	2-11502	48

The hotels in this category charge between US$6-16 for a single. I recommend seven hotels in this price range. Five of these are located near the Thamel area, but not in the area itself. They are thus within walking distance of many of restaurants which have opened in Thamel. One is near Durbar Square and the New Road and one is in Patan in quiet surrnundings.

Hotel Vajra is the more expensive and a good hotel in this price range. It is on the road from Thamel to Swayambhu Temple (Monkey Temple) and is a little away from the city centre. It is entirely new and caters to those who are interested in Tibet and Buddhism. One of the interesting attractions is the library in the hotel. Singles/doubles costs US$10/20. *Hotel Ambassador*, under the same name as the well known Kathmandu Guest House, is slightly more expensive and is located near the Indian and British embassies. *Hotel Nook* is centrally located at Kantipath, close to both Durbar Square and the Thamel area. It has long been popular with 'affluent' budget travellers. *Aloha Inn* is in the Jawlakhel area in Patan, in quiet surroundings. Many of its residents are in Nepal on UN assignments. There is also a beautiful garden. Singles/doubles are US$9/13. *Hotel Panorama*, again centrally located, is within a few minutes walking distance of New Road, the Post Office and old Kathmandu. Singles/doubles US$6/10. The *Tibet Guest House* in Chhetrapati area is five minutes' walk from Thamel and is run by Tibetans. People who have stayed here have found it to give good value. Singles/doubles are US$10/12. The building is entirely new.

Places to Stay – bottom end

Thamel Area Most low price hotels (below US$5 for a single) are found in the Thamel area which is about 15 minutes' walk from the centre of Kathmandu. From the city centre walk along Kantipath, the road north from New Road Gate towards the embassy area, turn left to the new Royal

Palace and two blocks further will bring you to Thamel. This area is more expensive than Freak Street.

A good place to stay here is *Kathmandu Guest House* (tel 2-13628) which is usually packed with voluntary workers and people travelling with overland bus companies. Even during the slack monsoon season it can be difficult to get a room in this popular hotel. There is a pleasant garden and parking space for cars and buses. Recently a London travel magazine called it one of the best places outside Europe and North America. Their prices have gone up in 1985 and the cheapest single now costs US$4.

One of the nicest hotels in Thamel, *Hotel Shakti* (tel 2-16121), has been built in a quiet garden setting. Singles with bath cost US$5. Recommended.

Hotel Star (tel 4-12100), next to the Kathmandu Guest House has long been popular with budget travellers and charges US$2/4 for bathless/with bath singles. *Hotel Asia* (tel 2-16541) charges US$3/6 for singles/doubles. It is a Nepalese house converted into a hotel.

Jyatha Area There are several bottom end hotels in this area, west of Kantipath and half way between Thamel and New Road. One advantage of staying here is that it is within walking distance of many interesting places.

Hotel Tushita (tel 2-16144) is on Kantipath and formerly housed the American Embassy. Singles/Doubles are US$4/6. *Hotel Kohinoor, Hotel Himalayan View* (tel 2-14890) and *Hotel Sunrise* (tel 2-16492) have US$5 singles and are quite Popular. One traveller found *Hotel Sunrise*, run by Tibetans, to have clean, large rooms and a helpful management.

Places to Stay – rock bottom

The wide range of hotels and lodges in this category offer excellent opportunities for good but inexpensive accommodation for low budget travellers. So many have opened recently that it is becoming increasingly difficult for the clientele, invariably students and young travellers to make a choice. The intense competition has led to the provision of some minimum facilities like hot showers. As hotels in this category do not have heating facilities in the winter, it is important to look for a room facing south so that you get sunlight into your room, or at least find a hotel with a garden or open space to enjoy the sunlight.

Most of the lodges in this category used to be in Freak Street, but many have now opened also in the Thamel area. Those in Thamel are likely to be more expensive than similar places elsewhere however. Besides, Freak Street is much quieter these days.

Freak Street In the heart of Freak Street is *Century Lodge* (2-15769), the best place in this price range, and in a quiet location off the main street. A single costs Rs 15 and hot showers cost Rs 2. There is also a library with many English books available. Bikes can be rented. Suman, the amiable manager, is a good source of information on interesting places to see in the valley. *Sayami Lodge* is a good cheap place where singles cost Rs 25. *Annapurna Lodge, Monumental Lodge* and *Temple Lodge* are also popular with many travellers.

Pie Alley Also known as Pig Alley, this street is actually called Maru Tole. This is where the famous pie shops of Kathmandu opened in the early '70s; only a few remain. *Camp Hotel*, one of the oldest hotels in Kathmandu, has recently been renovated. Doubles cost between Rs 35-50. *Yeti Lodge* in the same area charges Rs 10/18 for single/double and caters for those on the very bottom rocks.

Thamel Area A large number of very cheap lodges were opened in Thamel in the mid-'80s. *Om Guest House*, which charges Rs50/60 for single/double, is popular. *Yeti Cottage*, on the same street as Kathmandu Guest House has now become popular with overland bus companies as there is a large garden and parking space. Single/doubles cost Rs 25/50. There are three cheapies on the quiet street leading from Thamel to Chhetrapati (behind the High School). *Earth House Lodge* (tel 4-10050 is an old Nepalese house converted to a hotel and costs Rs 20/35 for single/double. On the same street, *Himal Cottage* charges only Rs 20 for singles and is run by nice people. *St Mnritz Cottage* is run by a Nepali who used to work in a lodge by the same name in Aspen, Colorado. Singles/doubles are Rs 30/40. There are also cheaper dormitories. *Garden Guest House* (tel 4-12987) charges Rs 55 a double and has a good sun roof. *Holy Lodge* is a traditional Nepalese home converted to a lodge (hence its narrow stairways). It is popular with Peace Corps volunteers. Singles/doubles are Rs 25/50.

Jawlakhel Area The only Youth Hostel in Nepal, *Mahendra Yuvalaya* (tel 5-21003) is in this area. Dormitories are Rs 7 a bed, singles between Rs 18-25. *Patan Guest House* at Man Bhawan in the same area is mainly partronized by ex-Gurkha soldiers from the British army. A double costs Rs 20.

Other Places One of the nicest cheap places to stay in Kathmandu, away from either Freak Street or Thamel, is *Kathmandu Lodge* (tel 2-13868) near Durbar Square. Singles are Rs 25. Popular with affluent budget travellers, people return to this place with monotonous regularity.

If you want to stay in a rural setting but still be within walking distance of Kathmandu city centre there is the newly opened *Hotel Catnap* in Chhauni, on the way to the Monkey Temple. The rooms are good and clean and offer a great view of Kathmandu city. Singles/double are Rs 35/45. *Ajima Guest House* (tel 2-16088) near the bus station in Bagh Bazaar is in an entirely new building and has a helpful management. Singles/doubles are Rs 25/30.

Renting a Room or Home

If you're planning to stay for an extended period, it is possible to rent a private home for as little as Rs 200 a month. Main areas are Swayambhu, Bodhnath or in Freak Street, although you can find long term accommodation in other area. A casual wander around Swayambhunath will usually turn up some place – or small children will locate you! There are various noticeboards which may have information about places to rent – the restaurant in Kathmandu Guest House, Rum Doodle, Aunt Jane's Place or the Peace Corps Office are just a few. It is often better to take over a place from a departing traveller to avoid having to find all the comforts of home eg. furniture. Also, as refrigerators are not readily available make sure you're near a market.

If you wish to rent rooms, apartments or houses (in all price ranges) you could try Mr Thapa at Jyatha Tol (tel 2-12472) of Thapa Real Estate (PO Box 438). He doesn't charge any commission to the leasee.

Where to Eat

Kathmandu's restaurants offer an amazing variety of foods. Most overland travellers find the food in Kathmandu to be better and more delicious than anywhere east of Istanbul. Where else in the middle of nowhere could you get sheesh kebab (Afghanistan), wiener schnitzel (German or Austrian), borsch (Russian), tandoori chicken (northern Indian), masala dosa (southern India), kothe (Tibetan), chow mien (Chinese), hamburgers, hot dogs, brownies and banana splits (American), spaghetti (Italian), chicken a la provencal and chateaubriand (French), enchiladas (Mexican), sukiyaki (Japanese) and dal bhat tarkari (Nepali)? Where else but Kathmandu?

Not only that, but Kathmandu's unique pie shops specialise in making pies and cakes, the quality of which approaches those available in the west. This is very surprising to a Kathmanduite who can remember when, in 1955, there was only one restaurant in all of Kathmandu! All this is indicative of the great changes that have taken place in Nepal since it ended its long isolation and flung is doors open to the world. The Tibetan refugees who entered Nepal during this period have been a strong factor in the development of Nepal as the mini-gastronomic paradise of south Asia; many of the Chinese and Tibetan restaurants are run by Tibetans. There are few places in the east where so many different dishes, from so many countries, can be found in so small a city.

Quality Restaurants

Expensive but excellent describes the *Yak and Yeti Chimney Room* which was originally started by Boris. Born in Russia, Boris formerly ran the Royal Hotel, the only high class hotel for westerners in Nepal during the 1950s. Undoubtedly one of the best restaurants in Nepal it is in an old Rana palace. The elaborately decorated hall has been converted into a dining room, and around the large open fire o a cold nigh the *Yak and Yeti* has plenty of atmosphere.

Situated in Lal Durbar, about three minutes walk from the Hotel de L'Annapurna, it is often very crowded. Most of the *Yak and Yeti's* clientele consists of well-off tourists, diplomats and a few affluent Nepalese, but some budget-minded tourists do venture in to sample the delights of Nepal's unique restaurant. If you wish to eat here without too much expense then try the Ukrainian borsch, which is always delicious. Other popular dishes include stroganoff at Rs 60, and a fish dish called bekti.

Perhaps the best Indian food to be found in Kathmandu is from *Kabab-e-ghar*, a restaurant situated in Durbar Marg, just outside the Hotel de L'Annapurna. The decor is very pleasant, it includes Indian miniatures of the Pahari style. Classical Indian music is played in the evenings and 'ghazals' are chanted in Urdu. Its speciality is chicken tandoori dishes, including *chicken peshwari* for Rs 40, which is eaten with the bread called *nan*.

The *Himachuli Room* of the Soaltee Oberoi Hotel serves some of the best food in Kathmandu. Among the more popular dishes are a typically Nepalese soup *alu tama*, for Rs 16, sliced chicken with bamboo shoots for Rs 45 and a tandoori-chicken-type Nepal dish called *Sekuwa* for Rs 51. The restaurant has impressive decor and contains wood carvings from Bhaktapur. There is also traditional Nepalese music played here. *Fresco Italian Restaurant*, alongside the swimming pool at Hotel Soaltee, is also well known for its Italian dishes.

The *Arniko Room* in Hotel de l'Annapurna has perhaps the best Chinese food

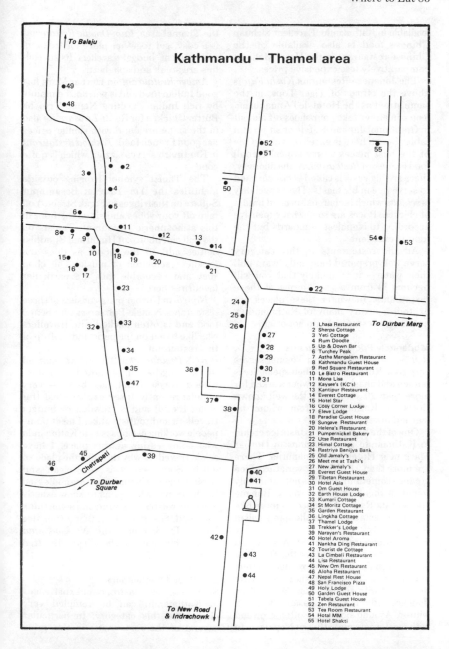

Kathmandu – Thamel area

↑ To Balaju

To Durbar Marg →

To Durbar Square ←

Chetrapati

To New Road & Indrachowk ↓

1 Lhasa Restaurant
2 Sherpa Cottage
3 Yeti Cottage
4 Rum Doodle
5 Up & Down Bar
6 Turchey Peak
7 Astha Mangalam Restaurant
8 Kathmandu Guest House
9 Red Square Restaurant
10 Le Bistro Restaurant
11 Mona Lisa
12 Kaysee's (KC's)
13 Kantipur Restaurant
14 Everest Cottage
15 Hotel Star
16 Cosy Corner Lodge
17 Eleve Lodge
18 Paradise Guest House
19 Sungave Restaurant
20 Helena's Restaurant
21 Pumpernickel Bakery
22 Utse Restaurant
23 Himal Cottage
24 Rastriya Banijya Bank
25 Old Jamaly's
26 Meet me at Tashi's
27 New Jamaly's
28 Everest Guest House
29 Tibetan Restaurant
30 Hotel Asia
31 Om Guest House
32 Earth House Lodge
33 Kumari Cottage
34 St Moritz Cottage
35 Garden Restaurant
36 Lingkha Cottage
37 Thamel Lodge
38 Trekker's Lodge
39 Narayan's Restaurant
40 Hotel Aroma
41 Nankha Ding Restaurant
42 Tourist de Cottage
43 La Cimbali Restaurant
44 Lisa Restaurant
45 New Om Restaurant
46 Aloha Restaurant
47 Nepal Rest House
48 San Francisco Pizza
49 Holy Lodge
50 Garden Guest House
51 Tabela Guest House
52 Zen Restaurant
53 Tea Room Restaurant
54 Hotel MM
55 Hotel Shakti

available in Kathmandu. Excellent Sichuan Chinese food is also available at the Chinese restaurant in the Hotel Malla at comparatively less expensive prices.

The Japanese Restaurant *Kushi Fuji* is above the offices of Tiger Tops, in the same street as the Hotel de l'Annapurna. You can either take your shoes off and sit in traditional Japanese style or sit up at a table. Lunch here is excellent value. One of the best places to try typical Nepali food is *Sunkosi Restaurant*. At the doorway, there are big vessels called *khadkalo* used to serve rice in big feasts. Their speciality is *sekuwa* which is charcoal-broiled breast of chicken. Prices are somewhat expensive according to Nepalese standards but the food is excellent.

All the restaurants in this category serve well-prepared food and always boil their water – it is unlikely that you will become ill from a visit to one of these restaurants. In winter these places are heated, a luxury many of Kathmandu's hotels and restaurants do not offer.

Moderately Priced Restaurants

Red Square Restaurant in Thamel serves very good Russian food. Their speciality is borsch and shaslik. The owner worked for more than 20 years with the well known Boris of Kathmandu from whom he learned his skills.

One of the best places to taste ice cream in Kathmandu is at *Niraulas* in Durbar Marg near Hotel de l'Annapurna. There are more than 21 different varieties of ice cream – something which is not commonly found in this part of the world. Banana splits costs Rs 15. The decor is more like in a chain restaurant on a shopping mall in the west.

The *Annapurna Coffee Shop* is located in the same compound as the Hotel de l'Annapurna and serves excellent coffee, and pastries. The coffee shop's walls are decorated with scenes showing Nepalese dancers and it is kept pleasantly warm in winter. Around noon it is often crowded with westerners and affluent Nepalese. In the Thamel area, *Rum Doodle Restaurant* is a cosy, get together place for trekkers and 'affluent' budget travellers. Its specialties are steak and spaghetti.

Amber Restaurant in Durbar Marg has good Indian food and is patronized mainly by rich Indians visiting Nepal. Try the Butter Chicken for Rs 30. *La Marmite* also in the same area and with similar prices has good French food. *Toshiba Restaurant* in Kantipath serves sizzler, which is quite good.

The Taoist symbol hanging outside identifies the *Yin Yang* at Basantapur Square on the fringes of Freak Street. You take off your shoes and sit on the floor in this atmospheric restaurant. Tankas on the wall and photos of Hindu and Buddhist deities add to the mood, as does the excellent selection of music. The chop suey and vegetable rolls are particular favourites here.

Nanglo in Durbar marg consists of three restaurants. Nanglo-Pub serves continental food and is often packed with travellers who like to eat on the patio and rooftop of this restaurant.

KC's Restaurant in Thamel was started by a long-haired, bearded Nepalese named Kaysee and has become very popular recently. It serves good steak (for about Rs 20) and is crowded by budget travellers and tourists alike. I meet many people working in embassies in Kathmandu who enjoy eating at this place. I have asked travellers why they like the place so much. Some say it is very clean and reminds them of home, others are impressed by the owner who seems to know exactly what the westerners want; and some think the food has become rather expensive lately. There's also the *Nanglo-China Room*, which has good noodles and stuffed dumplings.

Low Priced Restaurants

Some of the best gastronomic experiences in Kathmandu can be sampled very cheaply in this category. In particular several of the restaurants in this price range serve excellent Tibetan food the quality of which you'd have difficulty finding anywhere else in the world.

Most of the restaurants in this category are now located in the Thamel area. Many of the restaurants, formerly in Freak Street or Pie Alley 'relocated' in this area after the budget travellers started moving to Thamel area.

Thamel Area *Narayans Restaurant* has excellent Italian food and pies. Lasagna costs about Rs 30 and spring rolls are only Rs 15. It is often crowded out in the evenings, even during the off season. One of the most popular restaurants in this price range anywhere in Kathmandu. *Utse Restaurant* has been open for more than fifteen years and serves good quality Tibetan and Chinese food. It specializes in sweet and sour dishes and Tibetan *kothe* or *momo*. Recommended. *New Om Restaurant*, run by Tibetans, serves good Tibetan food. *Bistro Restaurant* has recently become very popular; try their quiches. *Nankha Ding* also specializes in Tibetan dishes, and has a more local atmosphere. *Kantipur Restaurant* serves good breakfast at good prices.

Cimbali Restaurant, on the way to the city centre, has good Italian dishes. Excellent pizzas are only Rs 15 to 20 and cappuccino coffee costs Rs 5.50. *San Francisco Pizza* also serves pizza but they're not like the ones I've had in New York.

Freak Street The *Lunch Box* is definitely the most popular Freak Street eating place – always packed with budget travellers. This place also has the best pies in Freak Street. *Kumari Restaurant*, next to Century Lodge, plays jazz and serves inexpensive good food. Try the Gateau Basque. The popular *Paradise Restaurant* serves vegetarian food.

Pie Alley Although this area used to have many restaurants and pie shops, not many remain. *Panchas Pastries* serves good

Italian and Continental food at inexpensive prices. Recommended.

Around New Road *Mom's Health Food* is on the street with the tree, off New Road. It serves health food similar to that in western vegetarian restaurants. Soya-burgers, soups, vegetables or fruit juices and excellent bread are all popular attractions. Nothing spicy here and you get honey instead of sugar in your tea. *Aunt Jane's Place*, started by the wife of the Director of Peace Corps in Nepal, used to be quite popular at one time. The food is still good.

Elsewhere If you're visiting Patan or the Tibetan Refugee Camp, *Blue Fox Restaurant* in Jawlakhel serves good momos and cakes. *Norling* and *Tso Ngong* in Kantipath area are two restaurants serving good Tibetan food. *Tripiti Restaurant* serves Indian thali-type dishes which are good.

Rock Bottom Restaurants
It is wise to be careful of hygiene in restaurants of this category although the ones listed here are adequately clean. There are also many good tea stalls and shops in this same price range that may not even have a name. The most popular meal in this group is probably *dal bhat tarkari*, the rice, lentil soup and vegetable everyday meal of most Nepalese. Most western travellers who have moved overland have been exposed to this kind of food for months and are quite used to it.

Lhasa Restaurant in Thamel has good Tibetan food at very inexpensive prices. The *New Tea Room* which used to be in Pie Alley has now moved to Thamel and serves inexpensive food.

There are more cheap restaurants in this category in the Freak Street area. *Lost Horizon* and *Dragon* are quite popular. Near the American Library in New Road *Shiva Bhojanalaya* serves thali-type cheap Indian food. One such thali including chappatis and rice costs Rs 10. There is also *Marwari Sewa Samiti* in the same area (near the Cinema) where you pay only Rs 7 for a thali all-you-can-eat dish. *Bangalore Coffee Hose* serves masala dosa.

Pie Shops and Snackbars

Kathmandu's amazing pie shops are not only one of the most memorable aspects of the city, they also serve very good pies. Only two remain in the area where it all started – in the Pie Alley area of Durbar Square. *Panchas Pastries* and *New Style* still dish up good pies and cakes. A large number of shops have opened elsewhere in town: *Narayans* in Thamel and *Lunch Box* in Freak Street are both excellent, especially their apple pies. *Bakers Cafe*, on the way to Thamel from New Road is a popular and often crowded shop. All these places are popular meeting spots for overlanders whose paths last crossed in Istanbul or Delhi.

One of the most pleasant and surprising aspects of Kathmandu is the interesting people one meets in the small restaurants and pie shops. This easy-going exchange of information seems more prevalent here than in most other cities on the way to the east.

Jim Wanless, USA

Niraulas in Durbar Marg serves 24 different kinds of ice cream and banana splits. *Sub Zero* in New Road also serves many different kinds of ice cream. It's in the same building as the Crystal Hotel. *Krishna Loaf Store* in Kamal Pokhari or *Nanglo* in Durbar Marg also serve excellent cakes, bread and rolls. *Pumpernickel Bakery* in Thamel serves excellent wholesome quality German bread and herbal tea. Milk, butter and Yak Cheese can be bought at the dairy branch on New Road or at the main dairy in Lainchaur near the British Embassy. If you are going trekking, take few kg of cheese along which costs Rs 64 per kg.

Eating & Drinking Do's & Don'ts

The time of year you're in Nepal determines whether you need to be very careful about the water you drink and the food you eat. During the dry tourist season from November to April you can drink tap water in Kathmandu, although it is definitely not advisable. During the wet monsoon season from May through September you should always insist on drinking boiled and filtered water. Lack of care can result in diarrhoea, dysentery or even hepatitis though most restaurants boil and filter the water as a matter of course. However, the point to remember is that just boiling the water is not enough. It has to be boiled continuously for at least 10 minutes to kill all the bacteria. Most restaurants in Nepal do not do that. Remember that tea is always boiled and, therefore, always safe.

When trekking the quality of the water is the single most important cause of stomach disorders. The golden rule is to only drink water from springs when you are positive that there is no human habitation upstream and to avoid drinking flowing water from rivers or streams. It is still better to boil and filter the water if possible. Above 1500 metres you need to be less careful than in the hotter climate at low altitudes.

As altitude increases, water's boiling point drops – so there is more chance of hardier bacteria (especially typhoid) surviving brief periods of boiling. I'd use sterilising tablets, most of which are chlorine based. I'd regard Nepal as a risky place for the health of the unwary.

Bob Day, England

It is generally quite safe to drink the Tibetan beer known as *chang* which is available very cheaply at places along many of the trekking routes or at Bodhnath and other locations in the valley. It is wise to avoid eating ice cream or any foodstuff sold outdoors, like from street vendors. In respectable restaurants ice cream is OK.

If you have any doubts about the quality of meat available in an unfamiliar restaurant then try to order egg dishes instead. Avoid eating meat while trekking unless you are carrying your own canned food or if you are certain that the chicken or goat has been freshly slaughtered.

Stomach Upsets If you are unfortunate enough to develop stomach problems in Nepal the best cure is to avoid solid food, drink only hot tea and let your body fight it naturally. If you decide to give it some help Lomotil and Mexaform tablets are both available in pharmacies in Kathmandu.

Popular Nepalese Food

chang – a mild alcoholic beverage made from barley, similar to western style beer.
thupka – Tibetan soup containing different kinds of meat.

momo or *kothe* – the Tibetan equivalent of ravioli or dim sums, consists of meat enclosed in dough then steamed or fried.
dal bhat tarkari – the typical Nepali meal consisting of lentil soup, rice and curried vegetables.
sikarni – a sweet dessert made from curd.
gundruk – a typical Nepalese soup made from dried vegetables.
tama – a dried bamboo shoot soup popular in Nepal.
buff – since Hindus can't eat beef, buff (water buffalo) is the normal substitute on many menus – buff steaks, buff noodle soup, even buffburgers.

If you develop a taste for chang and would like to brew some up at home here's the recipe. Get a five or 10 gallon fermenting vessel from a brewery supply shop. For the smaller vessel boil about two kg of millet for several hours. Millet swells considerably so make sure it has plenty of water and doesn't stick. When it cools add water to liquify it, you can also pass it through a blender to smooth it out. Then add burgundy yeast and the juice of a lemon and leave to ferment. This can take several weeks or a couple of months depending on taste. If you like a little extra kick to your chang add sugar, several kg, to the fermenting brew – this is really cheating since in Nepal sugar would be too expensive to be used in this way. The final product will have to be strained through a cloth and racked to remove the yeasty taste. This should not be taken as the only way to produce chang – experiment with it; in Bhutan for example they drink a chang made from half millet and half rice.

Recipe from Karel Tiller, Australia

Shopping

Many different souvenirs and handicrafts can be purchased in Nepal but it is important to shop around. Many items, such as the Tibetan and Chinese wood block prints, were not available at all in the late sixties but now are found in all the new shopping areas. Only government emporiums and a very few shops have fixed prices so the golden rule to remember when shopping is bargain! Usually the price first quoted will have a built-in bargaining margin.

Popular buys include:

Masks *Papier mache* masks of many different sizes are used for mask dancing which takes place in Kathmandu in September. Mask images include elephant-headed Ganesh, the terrifying Bhairab and the living Goddess Kumari. Almost all the souvenir shops in Kathmandu sell masks but the best place to buy them inexpensively is the small town of Thimi where they are actually made. Thimi is midway between Kathmandu and Bhaktapur; you can visit the mask painter Kansa Chitrakar on the old Kathmandu to Bhaktapur road about 15 minutes' walk from the bus stop. Prices range from Rs 5 to 30 depending on size. They make good wall decorations. Another good buy in Bhaktapur are the locally manufactured puppets.

Nepali Caps All Nepalese officials are required to wear Nepali caps – topi – when formally dressed. They're black in colour and made in Bhaktapur. Caps are a popular purchase because they look so typically Nepali. There is a cluster of shops selling nothing but caps in an area of old Kathmandu between Asan and Indrachowk; prices run from Rs 15 to 20.

Tibetan Handicrafts Tibetan prayer wheels are possibly the best known Tibetan handicraft: they make good presents to take home. Also popular are musical instruments, charm boxes, dorjes (thunderbolts) and other religious items. Bodhnath used to be a good place for Tibetan items but the large number of short-stay tourists who now rush out there on guided tours and indiscriminately buy anything at the first price asked have pushed prices up to absurd levels.

Tankas Colour paintings of the deities, called tankas, are painted by Tibetans or by Newars and Tamangs. Many are kept in monasteries but many of the *antique* tankas for sale in Kathmandu are artificially aged over a smoky fire. Tankas can be found for as little as Rs 50 while a good old one could easily cost over Rs 1000. There is no particular place to look for tankas although you will find many in shops at Bodhnath, around Freak Street and in Bhaktapur. There is a new shop in Bhaktapur, next to the recently renovated Pujahari Math monastery, where you can see the tankas being painted. I also found the prices of tankas to be more reasonable here compared to other places.

Everest Thanka in Thamel (on the road to Kathmandu Guest House) (tel 2-16007) has tankas which are somewhat better quality than those found in many other places at reasonably expensive prices. They also operate a school of scroll painter near the Temple of Pashupatinath where you can watch the painting being done. They have promised 10% off the price of any tanka to readers of this book.

Nepalese Handicrafts Patan, where many traditional handicrafts and bronze-works are manufactured, is the best place to go. Nepal is one of the few places in Asia where they make bronze by the 'lost wax process'. This is perhaps the most unique

A Khukri

The carpets usually cost from US$100 to US120 each. Their quality is better if wool from the highlands (Tibetan wool) is used. The carpets can be vacuumed, although you should ensure that the dyes are colourfast before buying. Tibetan carpets are vibrantly coloured and have striking designs, but were originally meant as wall hangings rather than floor coverings. The small square carpets are often made into seat cushions. The wood jackets, popularly known as *yakets*, seem to be worn by every visitor to Kathmandu.

Block Prints Block prints of Tibetan, Chinese and Nepalese deities are available in large numbers printed on local rice paper. Many shops around Thamel and Freak Street sell prints at prices from Rs 10 to 30. One of the better known places is *The Print Shop* which is in Thamel on the street that leads to Kathmandu Guest House. They also sell black and white and colour photographs of Nepal.

I would recommend a visit to the bead bazaar, within the main bazaar, north-west of Durbar Square. Here you can buy strings of many coloured beads very cheaply and also several thicknesses of materials to make rings and bracelets.

Annette Mahoney, England

feature of artwork in Nepal at present. A bronze statue may cost as little as Rs 150. There are now many small shops around Durbar Square in Patan. You can see handicrafts being made at the Patan Industrial Estate at Lagankhel, the prices here are quite low. The Government Emporium on New Road, Kathmandu, also charges fair, fixed prices but the choice is somewhat limited.

For good bargains in Nepalese or Tibetan curios go to the vendors who spread their wares on blankets in Basantapur or Durbar Square – but be prepared to bargain.

Tephen Frantz, USA

Tibetan Carpets, Jackets, Bags It is a good idea to visit the Tibetan refugee camp in Jawlakhel near Patan to see Tibetan carpets being woven. They are also available in the complex of narrow streets between Asan and the National Theatre.

Khukris The Nepalese knife, traditional weapon of Gurkha soldiers, can be bought for Rs 20 to Rs 500 depending on size and quality.

Nepalese Tea Tea is grown in Nepal in the far east of the country in the area bordering Darjeeling. It is claimed to be equal to the famous Darjeeling tea in quality. The best known teas are *Ilam* and *Mai Valley*, packets of which can be bought for about Rs 40.

Clothes Western women often like Tibetan and Nepalese garments. You'll find all sorts of clothes on sale around the Thamel and Freak Street areas. The traditional

Nepalese coats, overlapping at the front and closed with four ties, are another popular purchase – especially in the maroon velvet material from Pokhara.

Jewellery Jewellery of high and low quality is cheap to buy in Kathmandu and designs and carvings can be created to order. One popular buy is a red bead necklace containing a gold ornament known as 'Tilhari'. Worn by almost all married women in Nepal, it serves the same purpose as a ring in the west. The best place to look for a *Tilhari* is in the Indrachowk area near Durbar Square.

It will cost you very little to have a Nepalese jeweller working on the street make some article in silver or stone.

BB, France

Terra Cotta A wide variety of attractive terra cotta pots, bowls and flowerpots are made – those shaped like an elephant are favourites. Several shops near Indrachowk sell them. They are made in Thimi.

Other The latest buys include lamp shades of different forms and batik paintings available in Freak Street which were not common before.

Nepal is having, in common with many other Asian countries, a major problem of theft of works of art from temples and monasteries. Many of these masterpieces end up in museums of private collections in America or Europe. If you visit Dhulikhel you can walk down to the temple at the foot of the hill and see the three small pairs of feet that are all that remain of the statues which used to stand in the temple.

Should you buy a work of art which could be more than one hundred years old it is necessary to get permission from the Department of Archaeology before you take it out of the country. If in doubt check – the office is in the National Archives Building (tel 12778), just two blocks from Immigration. Hours are 10 am to 5 pm, but if you go by 1 pm you can expect approval by the same evening. To be on the safe side go there a few days before you depart, customs checks are much more severe on exit than entry to the country.

Each time I visit Kathmandu I take a new pair of jeans with me and get a dragon embroidered on the cuffs. There are a host of little embroidery shops around Kathmandu and they'll produce a brilliant design remarkably quickly and cheaply. Make sure you remember which little shop it was, though. I really thought I'd lost my jeans once!

Tony Wheeler, Australia

Getting it all back Home Unless you are sure about their reliability it is best not to leave articles to be mailed by the shop where you purchased them. There have been instances when articles have never arrived; unfortunately this is also true of some packing companies – I recommend *Sharma and Sons Packers and Movers* in Kantipath (tel 12709). You could also mail your stuff from the Foreign Post Office. For a small fee there are people who will help you pack.

Living in Kathmandu

Cultural Programmes

Even if your visit to Nepal is not during the festival season you can still enjoy Nepalese dance and music in Kathmandu. At the National Theatre there are Nepalese operas and musicals almost every day. In addition programmes of folk dancing are put on by:

Everest Cultural Society (tel 2-15429) shows Nepalese folk dances every evening at 7 pm, the one-hour show costs Rs 50. Dances from the Sherpa highlands, from the Newars of the valley and from other ethnic groups are shown, including the Yak dance, Peacock dance, Mask dance and Witch Doctor dance.

Lalupate presents Nepalese folk dances from a variety of ethnic groups at 6 pm every day at Hotel shanker, admission is Rs 35. There is also a free performance of Nepalese folk dance at Hotel Soaltee Oberoi's Himalchuli Restaurant every evening.

On Monday nights you can hear the traditional Nepalese music in a temple a few blocks off New Road in Asantol. Wait for the religious ceremony to end at about 9.30 and just sit in the arcade entrance to the temple and watch the warming up of the musicians. It is done with a large chillum and the music begins when the coughing stops.

Peter Thompson, USA

Libraries

Kathmandu has an interesting choice of libraries set up by the Americans, British, French, Germans, Russians, Chinese and Indians. Not only can you read recent journals, newspapers and books but there are also film nights.

The *French Cultural Centre* (tel 14326) has a good selection of French publications and is open from 9 to 7 pm on weekdays. There are also film nights which cost Rs 5 for admission. More than 100 French films are shown during the course of the year. The centre is located in Bagh Bazaar opposite the bus stand to Bhaktapur.

Located near the post office and the tower, the *Goethe Institute* (tel 2-15528) has a reading room open from 4 to 7 pm daily. Films are shown fairly frequently and there is also an active Nepal-Deutsch club.

The *US Library and Information Service* is on New Road and is open from 11 am to 7 pm Monday to Friday if you want to keep up with *Time* and *Newsweek*. Recent changes in the regulations allow only Nepalese and foreign residents in Nepal to use the library. The *British Council* (tel 2-11305) is on Kantipath and is open from 11 am to 6 pm Sunday to Friday.

'Rastriya Pustakalaya' or 'Nepal National Library' at Pulchok in Patan has books in English, Sanskrit and Indian languages. A large number of the books in the library were collected by the Royal Preceptor in Nepal who had been awarded the title of 'jewel of head of scholars' by the King of Nepal. The Tribhuvan University Library of Kirtipur has a nice collection of books and resembles a library in an American university. It is open Sunday to Friday from 9 am to 6 pm.

The Kaiser Library (worth visiting for the building), near the new Royal Palace, has an incredible collection of books, many on Buddhism, Tibet and Nepal that I have never seen before.

Hester Ross, USA

Research Work

If you are undertaking research on economic, social or anthropological aspects of Nepal, the best place to contact is the International Research and Consulting Centre, PO Box 1577, Kathmandu. You can also phone Mr Sharad Sharma on 2-13438.

Legal Work

Nepal Law Firm (tel 2-11710) in Ram Shah Path has English speaking lawyers who could assist you if you have any legal problem in Nepal.

Finding Employment in Nepal

Western visitors often wonder if it is possible to find work in Nepal. The answer is, it is very difficult but not impossible. It is easier for those having English as their mother tongue. There are many privately-owned schools in Nepal and they often require trained teachers or just English-speaking adults to teach. Last year, I met a Dutch teacher who wanted to work in Nepal. He visited 15 schools and five of them were willing to hire him. But don't get the impression that it is too easy. The pay is minimal – between US$50 to US$100 a month, however it is cheap to live in Nepal. Finding work in a school might help solve the visa problem, but it takes a very long time to get things done. Technically, no work permit is required by foreigners and the main problem is getting a visa extension. Apart from schools, there are many aid missions, travel agencies, consulting firms and airline offices which could be worth approaching. But the number of such openings is small so your chances of getting them would be very remote. This does not mean that its impossible or not worth trying.

Learning Nepali

If you want to learn Nepali from the same instructors who teach Peace Corps Volunteers who work in Nepal, contact Mr Cheej Shrestha at Nazal (near the Lhotse Hotel) or telephone him at 12551. The charges are Rs 25 to 30 per hour. Another good place is *Training Service Centre* (tel 15926) in Thamel which has similar prices. Nepali is a relatively easy language to learn and a working knowledge could be obtained in three to eight weeks.

Astrologer

If you would like to consult a Nepalese astrologer, there is one person who has a good reputation, whom many westerners have visited. He is Mangal Raj Joshi (tel 2-21159) who lives in Patan near Kathmandu.

Yoga

If you want to learn Yoga while in Kathmandu, there is a place called Arogya Ashram (tel 4-10776) at Battisputali near the temple of Pashupati. They teach different postures (including standing on the head) and 'Pranayama'. The Community Services Program run by the americans at Phora Durbar (tel 2-12593) offers courses on Yoga which cost Rs 200 a month.

Cinemas

Indian films, usually not subtitled, are the usual cinematic fare in the valley although there are occasional English language films. Kathmandu has four cinemas and there are also cinemas in Patan and Bhaktapur. Admission charges range from Rs 3 to Rs 10.

If you do not catch one in India, I suggest a Hindi movie. Even if you do not understand Hindi it will be an interesting, artistic experience. The nicest theatre is near the Palace and Chinese Embassy, price is less than Rs 4.

Bill Cook, USA

Media

The *Rising Nepal* is the main English daily and covers most news from abroad but can be difficult to find if you don't get hold of a copy early in the morning. *Radio Nepal* has English news bulletins at 8 am and 8.30 pm daily. *Time* and *Newsweek* are readily available in Nepal. You can buy the latest issues at the store opposite the big tree in New Road, where Indian dailies such as *The Statesman* or the *Times of India* are also available. The daily *International Herald Tribune* is also available in many shops.

Bookshops

Kathmandu has a surprising variety of

quite good bookshops with particularly interesting selections of books on Nepal – many of which are not available outside the country. There are bookstalls in the main hotels in old Kathmandu and around Freak Street. Probably the best selection of books in Kathmandu is at *Educational Enterprises* near New Road Gate or *Ratna Book Distributors* at Bagh Bazaar. Both have showrooms. Recently several new bookstores have opened in the street around the Clock Tower and National Theatre. Actually, there are more than seven bookstores in the one street – from the National Theatre to the Clock Tower and further east to Bagh Bazaar these include: *Everest Book Store, Annapurna Book Service* and *Himalayan Booksellers* all have a good collection of books on Nepal. In Thamel, the *Order of Pilgrims* has a collection of rare books on Nepal and Tibet.

For selling books, try the *Kathmandu Trade Post* run by an ex-police officer in Freak Street or *Tantric Bookstore*. There is also *Librarie Francaise* in Kantipath which sells books in French.

Visit the Chinese books store located in the bazaar area off Indrachowk. They have beautifully illustrated story books and water colour prints, some in English. They also have interesting sets of postcards, reprints of water colour paintings, glimpses of cities, at an extraordinarily cheap price. Ask to see all the different photos of Mao.

Kathleen Bannon, USA

Swimming

The Swimming Pool in the five star Yak and Yeti Hotel is open to outsiders and costs Rs 35 per day. It also has a cheaper rate if you become a member and are staying longer.

During summer, it is possible to swim at the pool at the National Stadium (opposite Telegram Office) for Rs 5 a day. It is open from 10 am to 5 pm. Monday is especially reserved for women. The swimming pool

at Balaju Water Gardens is likely to be quite crowded in the summertime. *Narayani Hotel* also has a swimming pool which is open to non-residents for Rs 30 per day. The pools at Soaltee and Annapurna Hotels are only open to residents and their guests.

Nightlife in Kathmandu

Many restaurants and snack bars in Kathmandu are so crowded that they make good places to meet Nepalese and other westerners, but there are few discos or nightclubs as they are known in the west. In Kathmandu, people go to bed quite early and in winter you hardly see anyone on the streets after 10 pm. Besides, many visitors are not particularly worried by the lack of night life, it's not what they have come this far for – so the many places that have opened in the past few years have not all had a long or successful life.

For most people, a German visitor's comments sum it up; 'If you want night life in Kathmandu, you have to make your own.'

Nevertheless there are some places:

The Soaltee Oberoi Casino – for something to do at night. Black Jack, pontoon and a roulette wheel – you might even come away a few rupees richer. Even if you do not like gambling the music is good and it is fun to watch.

Usan Ulkina, USA

There are free buses to the casino from all the leading hotels of Kathmandu from 8 to 11 pm. If you gamble, free drinks are also served. Some hotels also distribute US$5 coupons free which can be exchanged to play at the casino. The Soaltee is one of the very few casinos in this part of the world. You can play in Indian Rs or US$ and take the money out of the country if you win.

There is band music and ballroom dancing in many of the luxury hotels in Kathmandu. In the last decade, several discos opened but could not survive very long. The ones that are still open are making it more difficult for non-tourist men to enter, as there is often a surplus of this group. *Copper Floor Disco* (tel 4-13304) near Hotel Lali Guras at Lazimpat is quite popular.

The Terai

All travellers who enter Nepal overland from the south pass through the Terai on their way to Kathmandu or Pokhara. Few spend much time in the region, however. Such towns as Birganj, Bhairawa, Janakpur are all located in the Terai.

THE TERAI

Besides being the 'granary' of Nepal, the Terai also contains Lumbini, Buddha's birthplace, and the Chitwan National Park where wildlife of the area including the one-horned rhinos can be seen. After the recent opening of the road connecting the Terai with the Kathmandu-Pokhara Highway, both of the above attractions are now so near Sunauli or Narayanghat that they are only a couple of hours away from the main travel route of overland travellers.

The Terai consists of the 'Outer Terai' which is flat and is an extension of the Gangetic Plains; and the 'Inner Terai' which is surrounded by hills in the south and is actually a valley. The Terai extends the length of Nepal, except in two regions where it only contains the Inner Terai. Much of the Terai was heavily forested till the 1960s when the eradication of malaria resulted in mass migration from the hills causing large scale deforestation. A substantial portion of the Terai, especially along the northern foothills, still contains large Sal forests. The Terai also contains most of the industries of Nepal, and produces more than half of the country's GDP and government revenue.

Most of the people in eastern and central Terai have close ethnic and linguistic ties with the Indians across the border in the states of UP and Bihar. The recent migration of the people from the hills has changed the ethnic character of the Terai. It is also a region of Nepal which has developed more than the hilly region in general. Almost two-thirds of the Terai contains good, motorable roads connecting Kathmandu and the Indian border and almost all of its towns have electricity laid on.

BHAIRAWA

The city of Bhairawa is a convenient point for an overnight stay if you are planning to visit Lumbini, Buddha's birthplace. It is the headquarters of a small Terai district and contains banks, government offices and hotels. As there are frequent bus services to Lumbini, and everything of interest in Lumbini can be seen in a few hours, it is better to overnight in Bhairawa than in Lumbini.

The best hotel in Bhairawa is Lumbini Hotel (tel 271) but it does not seem to be well managed these days. Singles/doubles are Rs 110/170 including breakfast. Hotel Himalayan Inn (tel 347) is cheaper as singles are only Rs 65. It's popular with overland bus companies and affluent budget travellers. There are cheaper hotels around the city centre which charge about Rs 25/35 for doubles. These include Hotel Kailash and Shambala Guest House. Pashupati Lodge is in a similar price range and is popular with Indian travellers. There are also very cheap overnighting places at the border town of Sunauli; these are very basic. Two are Mamata Lodge and Jai Vijay Lodge, of which the latter plays loud western music in its restaurant.

LUMBINI

A 22-km road connecting Bhairawa with Lumbini, the birthplace of Buddha, has recently been completed. There is a bus service every two hours during the day to Lumbini which costs Rs 5 but means waiting more than an hour as the bus travels very slowly. A taxi from Bhairawa costs about Rs 300 for the round trip, including a couple of hours at Lumbini. Although there are some hotels in Lumbini,

Top: Wheels from a temple chariot in Bhaktapur
Left: Temple struts on the Jagnath Temple in Durbar Square, Kathmandu
Right: Children in Kirtipur

Out of the valley
Top: Bridge at Kodari on the Chinese border
Bottom: Buddha carving at Namobuddha

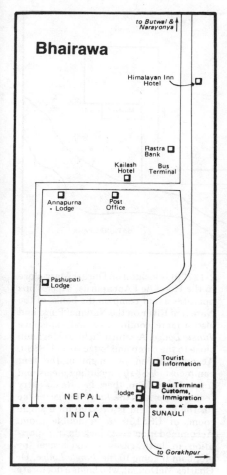

Bhairawa

to Butwal & Narayonya

Himalayan Inn Hotel

Rastra Bank

Kailash Hotel

Bus Terminal

Annapurna Lodge

Post Office

Pashupati Lodge

Tourist Information

Bus Terminal Customs, Immigration

NEPAL   lodge

INDIA   SUNAULI

to Gorakhpur

These include the ancient Ashoka Pillar, the temple of Buddha's mother Maya Devi and the tank where she took a bath before she gave birth to Buddha. There is also excavation work which recently unearthed two chaityas dating back to the 3rd century BC.

The Tibetan monastery, established in 1975, has interesting paintings on the walls and a huge bronze image of the Buddha which was set up by a Raja from Mustang (a region in northern Nepal). There is also a Buddhist monastery with a white Buddha donated by the Burmese, a huge tanka painting and wood carvings on the gate. The ancient Chinese traveller Huen Sang found the Ashok Pillar, Maya Devi Temple, some chaityas and a bathing tank which can all be seen now. Although the Muslims form a small minority in Nepal, it is surprising that most of the villages around Lumbini are predominantly Muslim. The entire Lumbini region is expected to be developed, with UN assistance, over the next few years.

The *Lumbini Guest House* is about the only place to stay here. You can probably knock their price of Rs 100 for a double down to about Rs 70, which is still expensive. Food here is also rather pricey and there's not much available. The rooms, however, are clean and very comfortable and there are pleasant gardens and lawns.

CHITWAN NATIONAL PARK
A visit to the park should not be missed as it is one of the finest wildlife experiences in Asia (including the chance to see the one-horned rhinos), and because the park is so easily accessible.

The best season to visit the park is between March and May when the elephant grass is cut and the game can be seen more easily. However, it can be very hot in May. October-February is also a good season.

Though they never went to Kathmandu many Europeans, including King George V and the Prince of Wales, visited

it is better to stay in Bhairawa as there is not much to see there. Most travellers prefer to stay in Bhairawa and make a day trip to Lumbini.

In 249 BC, when he had been king for about 20 years, King Devanam Pryadarshin, better known as the Emperor Ashoka, came to Lumbini to worship at the Buddha's birthplace and to erect a giant pillar. The main sight-seeing attractions in Lumbini can all be seen in a few hours.

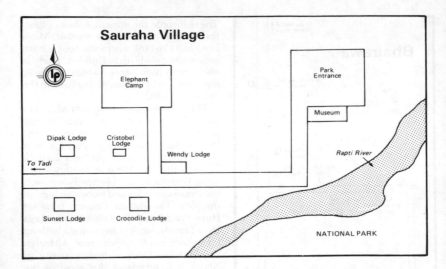

Sauraha Village

Chitwan in the early part of this century to hunt game.

The entrance to the park is in Sauraha. There is also a small museum where there are park-related exhibits. Several cheap lodges such as *Elephant Camp* are in the village of Sauraha while *Gaida Wildlife Camp* is actually in the park – but only just. *Tiger Tops* and *Chitwan Jungle Lodge* are located in the western and eastern parts of the park.

There are several ways of visiting Chitwan National Park. For those with a lot of money to spend, *Tiger Tops Hotel Complex* is connected by air from Kathmandu. It is luxurious and expensive, and can cost more than US$150 a day. The more moderate hotels are within an hour's drive from the city of Narayanghat, which is on the overland route from the Indian border to Kathmandu. These are less than half as expensive as Tiger Tops. It is also possible to visit the park on the cheap for as little as US$15 a day.

Tiger Tops

The Tiger Tops jungle camp is located in the Chitwan Valley 130 km south-west of Kathmandu. The office of Tiger Tops (tel 2-12706) is located on Durbar Marg close to the Hotel de l'Annapurna. Tiger Tops operates a tent camp on the banks of the Narayani River on the National Park, and also a more comfortable and expensive *Jungle Lodge*. A return flight to Meghauli close to the camp and lodge costs US$80. Accommodation per night in the tent camp costs US$100 including meals and tours. In addition, there is a Rs 65 entry fee to the park. In the *Jungle Lodge* the fee for the first night is US$200 for a single room, or US$150 for a double room. Accommodation costs include transportation in both cases – you travel by elephant if going to the *Jungle Lodge*. Dr Charles McDougal, who holds a doctorate in anthropology and is an authority on the people and wildlife of Nepal, gives lectures on the area and the animals in the park. A new addition to the activities at Tiger Tops is the village, which shows how indigenous people of the area, known as Tharus, live.

Tiger Tops Lodge – Tiger Tops, PO Box 242 Kathmandu – Telex NP 216 TIGTOP – Kathmandu office tel 12706 – 20 rooms all with bath – bar – restaurant.

In the park there is opportunity for boating and canoeing, visits to native villages, fishing for mahseer in season, nature walks and treks, elephant treks, swimming and, of course, wildlife observation. Unlike African animals which tend to move in large herds, Asian wildlife is more solitary and shy. Observing wildlife involves patience and searching, but animals you may see include various deer, the sloth bear, wild boar, fresh water dolphins, crocodiles (careful where you swim), the rare Great Indian one-horned rhinos, leopards and, with a good deal of luck, the very rare and elusive Royal Bengal tiger. Best season for visiting the park is from October to March when the weather is not too hot. Hunting is strictly prohibited. It is estimated that there are 400 rhinos and 30 tigers in the park, which is only a third of the number 25 years ago. Tiger Tops can also be reached after a two day raft trip on the Trisuli and Narayani Rivers. The trip starts at Mugling on the Kathmandu-Pokhara Highway and reaches Tiger Tops the following day after camping along the river bank.

Less Expensive ways of visiting the Park

There are two less expensive ways of visiting the park. If you stay in one of the three tourist class hotels inside or outside the park you will spend about US$200 for two nights (three days) including almost everything – which is about half the cost of Tiger Tops. The lodges have their own elephants and a ride costs no extra. Also, the lodges have their own trained naturalists who speak good English and have a good knowledge of the local flora and fauna. Alternatively, you can visit the park more cheaply on your own if you stay in one of the half dozen new lodges which have opened just outside the entrance to the park in the village of Sauraha. These, while cheap, offer a basic level of accommodation and only one has hot showers. You'll also have to find your own guide to visit the jungle. If you're pressed for time, this may not be the best option.

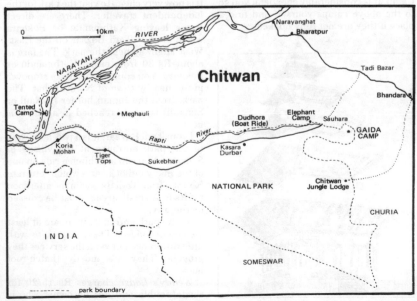

Elephant Camp is located in Sauraha near Tandi Bazaar in the Chitwan National Park (on the highway between Narayanghat and Hetaura). Guests stay in huts by the side of the Rapti River and pay US$180 which includes round trip transportation from Kathmandu, two nights' room and board, elephant rides and canoeing. It does not include National Park entrance fee and 10% tax. It is also open in the summer and monsoon from the end of May to mid-September. As this is off-season it is cheaper and cost US$130 per person for a tour. The camp also organizes a cultural program consisting of music and dance by the local Tharu villagers. Its manager Doug is an ex-Peace Corps volunteer who speaks fluent Nepali. It also has an office at Durbar Marg (tel 2-13976). *Gaida Wildlife Camp*, in the same area, charges US$160 for two nights' accommodation and food, elephant rides, etc. If you add round trip transport charges, the total cost is US$214 which is slightly more expensive than Elephant Camp. It is considerably cheaper if you go to the above camps yourself and find a place if they are not fully booked.

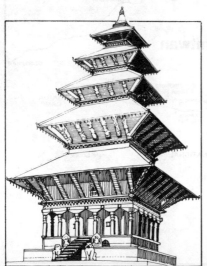

A new hotel called *Chitwan Jungle Lodge* has recently been opened on the eastern part of the park in the middle of dense forest. The wildlife in the eastern part is relatively less disturbed as it is away from the main entrance to the park and the other hotels and lodges. They charge US$195 for two nights stay which includes room and board, elephant rides and roundtrip transport from Kathmandu. There is a better possibility of viewing leopards and tigers from this location. With the exception of Tiger Tops, you get the feeling of really being inside the jungle when you stay in this lodge.

Visiting the park and the nearby village of Sauraha is a very special experience. The scenery is gorgeous with the Himalayas in the distance (in the winter). I found the village, largely inhabited by indigenous Tharu people, very interesting.

Edith Jones, USA

The Park on the Cheap
It is now very cheap to visit the park for the independent traveller. There are direct buses leaving Kathmandu or Pokhara which stop at Tadi Bazaar on the East-West Highway near the park. The fare is about Rs 30 from either Kathmandu or Pokhara. You could also make a stopover in the nearby town of Narayanghat. The park, from the Indian border (Raxaul or Sunauli) is easily reached in about four hours.

From Tadi Bazaar, it is a two-hour walk to the park entrance at the village of Sauraha. You can also hitch a ride on one of the many bullock carts which return to Sauraha from Tadi Bazaar in the afternoon for Rs 5. A small stream must be crossed on the way.

At the park entrance, there are at least six cheap lodges. These are quite with little difference between the services they provide. They are mostly thatch-roof huts.

Wendy's Lodge charges Rs 15/20 for single/double and has an owner who is friendly and speaks good English. *Sunset Lodge* is more spacious and is the latest addition. *Cristobal, Peacock* and *Crocodile* are also similar. *Rabu Ram Cottage*, expected to re-open soon, is also okay. The cheapest is *Dipak Lodge* which charges Rs 15 for a double.

The entrance to the park cost Rs 65 and is valid for one day. Elephant rides have become rather expensive lately at Rs 200 per person per hour. But you are almost certain to view at least a few rhinos if you go on elephantback. It isn't necessary to go inside the park to see a rhino; you can rent elephants outside at a cheaper price though these are not allowed into the park. There are watch towers inside the park but you're not permitted to overnight in these.

Many of the cheap lodges have English-speaking guides who are just teenage boys without formal training but they know the jungle and the wildlife surprisingly well. They will take you inside the park for 'jungle walks' for about three hours and charge Rs 25. Some of the better guides are Shiva of Wendy's, and Krishna from Cristobal Lodge. You should not walk in the forest without a guide as it could be dangerous. There have been reports of solitary travellers chased by rhinos inside the park. Even when you go with a guide for a jungle walk there is still some risk. Dusk and dawn are the best times for animal watching.

The park authorities also arrange boat rides along the Rapti River which forms the main boundary of the park. It costs Rs 25 for a one-hour ride; to buy tickets go early in the morning as the seat numbers are limited. This ride used to be a good way of seeing the many crocodiles before the devastating flood of 1984 washed most of them away.

TOWNS OF THE TERAI

Most travellers from the West are not specifically interested in the towns of the Terai (or Inner Terai), although they may pass through on their way from Darjeeling

or the Indian border to Kathmandu. Many of the towns seem similar to the towns in the Gangetic Plains in northern India.

Narayanghat (or Narayangarh) is located on the banks of River Narayani which is one of the three biggest in Nepal and drains the central part of Nepal. A large bridge has just been constructed over the river creating a vital link with the East-West Highway of Nepal. Narayanghat, along with its sister city of Bharatpur, is the administrative and commercial centre of the rich agricultural area of Chitwan, which was largely settled by people from the hills in the 1960s. Some of its original inhabitants, the *Tharus* still live here. It is also the gateway to the Chitwan National Park. A large fair takes place every year in mid-January in a town called Deoghat a few km north of Narayanghat. Tens of thousands of pilgrims gather to bathe in

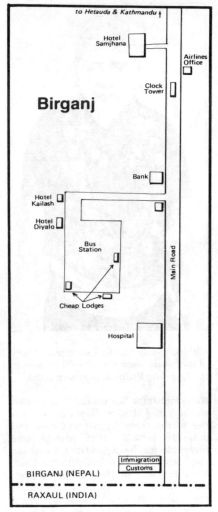

Birganj

to Hetauda & Kathmandu ↑

Hotel Samjhana

Airlines Office

Clock Tower

Bank

Hotel Kailash

Hotel Diyalo

Bus Station

Main Road

Cheap Lodges

Hospital

Immigration
Customs

BIRGANJ (NEPAL)

RAXAUL (INDIA)

town is growing very fast. If you want to stay overnight, *Hotel Chitwan* (tel 200) charges Rs 75 for a double. It's located on the road to Bharatpur and has parking space for vehicles.

Birganj This border town was, a few years ago, the main entry point to Nepal from India. It has lost its importance as more routes into the country have opened up. If you enter Nepal from Raxaul in India you will almost certainly have to spend a night in Birganj.

Almost all of the cheap lodges are found around the bus station. The *Amrapali, Tourist* and *Delicious* are among the better ones – they are quite similar and charge around Rs 12 for a single without bath. *Hotel Diyalo* is somewhat better and single rooms cost from Rs 36. The *Samjhana Hotel* is situated away from the centre of town and is patronised mainly by overland buses and motorists who require parking space. A single room here costs Rs 30 or you can camp for Rs 5.

Janakpur This town, located in eastern Terai, is famous historically as the birthplace of Sita of the epic Ramayana. There is a temple of Rama and Sita in the town which attracts many pilgrims. It also has a cigarette factory built in the 1960s with aid from the USSR. The local language is known as Maithili, which is also spoken in North Bihar in India.

Biratnagar is the second largest city in Nepal and the largest in the Terai. Being the centre of the jute industry, it is also the major industrial city in Nepal.

Dharan is situated on the foothills in the eastern Terai and is inhabited by people who migrated from the hills. It also has a camp for Gurkha soldiers in the British Army.

the holy waters where the rivers merge to become Narayani. Because of the opening of the new road connecting the Indian border with Kathmandu and Pokhara this

Pokhara

If the work of human beings has impressed you in the Kathmandu Valley it will be the work of nature which will cast a lasting spell on your visit to Pokhara. The skyline is dominated by the Annapurna range and the perfectly shaped peak of Macchapuchhare, the fish-tail mountain. The Himalayas seem much closer than they do in Kathmandu. A member of a mountaineering expedition, speaking of the view from Pokhara, said:

Compared to that vision, the Matterhorn would have looked crude, the peerless Weisshorn a flattened hump.

Toni Hagen, the Swiss geologist who, in the late fifties, was the first foreigner to travel extensively in Nepal, described the view from Pokhara:

Nepal is a land of contrast. Nowhere is this more clearly seen than here in Pokhara ... in the background, with no intermediate range between, the Annapurna chain rises abruptly to an altitude of over 8000 metres.

The Pokhara Valley contains three lakes, Phewatal, the most beautiful and accessible, is only about 15 minutes' walk from the airport; the others are Rupa and Begnas. The hills around Pokhara are inhabited largely by Gurungs – a tribal people who form one of the important constituents of the Gurkha rifles in both the Indian and British armies. Picturesque Gurung villages like Ghandruk and Siklis are within a few walking days of Pokhara and are really worth the effort to visit. The population of the valley itself consists largely of Brahmins and Chetris. The tradition of providing Gurkha soldiers from this area means that Pokhara has long been open to outside influence but there is still much population pressure from the surrounding hills. The salaries and pensions received from employment outside – through the army or Indian households – helps to improve conditions in this food deficient area.

The area around Pokhara is currently changing very rapidly. The construction of the road linking Pokhara to the Indian border and to Kathmandu – previously it was accessible only by flying or walking – has a major impact on the area. Pokhara is also the growth centre for mid-western Nepal in the country's four region development programme.

Pokhara is about 700 metres lower than Kathmandu and as a result rather warmer and more pleasant in late autumn and winter. On the other hand it is not a good place to visit in the monsoon as Pokhara gets twice the rainfall of Kathmandu.

GETTING TO POKHARA

There are bus and minibus services between Kathmandu and Pokhara and from there to the Indian border. Public buses from Kathmandu can be found at the foot of the Bhimsen Tower near the Post Office or at the bus stand near the City Hall. The buses leave in the early morning and it is advisable to reserve tickets at least a day in advance, cost is only Rs 35. These are the same kind of public buses that make the trip up from the Indian border. They are not very comfortable and you may have difficulty in stretching your legs.

More comfortable, although slightly more expensive, are the minibuses which are usually ex-overland vehicles. On these buses the cost if Rs 50 and tickets are sold from offices around Freak Street or in hotels. An advantage of travelling by minibus is that they will take you to the lake area of Pokhara. The public buses only go as far as the airport/bus stand from where it is expensive to get a taxi to the lake or entails a half hour walk. The

View of Himalayan Ranges from Pokhara

buses will also pick you up from the lake area for the return trip. It takes five or six hours to travel between the two towns.

There are frequent flights between Kathmandu and Pokhara; the short flight offers good Himalayan views and costs Rs 518. If you decide to travel by road, there are few dangerous curves, steep ascents or descents along the excellent Kathmandu-Pokhara highway.

Kathmandu-Pokhara Highway

The Kathmandu-Pokhara highway is 202 km long and for the most part follows the courses of three major rivers – the Trisuli, Marsyangdi and the Seti and crosses over two rivers – the Madi and Marsyangdi. The portion from Naubise, where the road to the Indian border splits off, is 176 km long and was constructed with Chinese assistance. When completed in the early seventies it had cost approximately 14 million.

From the fertile valley of Naubise, the road follows the small stream of Mahesh Khola for 22 km to its junction with the Trisuli River at Galchi Bazaar. The road then follows the Trisuli River through Gajuritar and Benighat, where the big Bidhi Gandaki River joins the Trisuli from the north to the confluence of the Marsyangdi and Trisuli at Mugling. This is the halfway point and a popular lunch stop; at an altitude of only 280 metres it is also the lowest point along the highway. The Chinese have also built a road leading south from Mugling to the Chitwan Valley where Tiger Tops is located. The sacred Hindu temple of Mankamana is only a few km away on the top of a steep hill.

Go to Bandipur, a beautiful Newar town, just off the Kathmandu-Pokhara Road. Before the road was built, it was a major trade centre of western Nepal. Its bazaars still show the prosperity of those times – multi-storeyed houses, a stone paved road and temples. The view of Annapurna and Machhapuchhare from the town is excellent. Get off the bus at Dumre and climb two hours.

David Jarmail, USA

One of the longest suspension bridges in Nepal crosses the Trisuli from Mugling and follows the course of the Marsyangdi. The combination of these two rivers is known as the Gandak, one of the major tributaries of the Ganges. About an hour from Mugling the road passes Dumre, a new town settled after the construction of the highway. Just above it on a hilltop is the beautiful town of Bandipur. The capital of the principality of Gorkha, where the unification of Nepal began, is north-east of this area in the hills. The road then continues through Damauli – the district headquarters which has a good-sized bazaar – across the Madi River by a big bridge and on to Khaireni, headquarters of an agricultural extension project being implemented with assistance from West Germany. Improved seed and fertilisers are being provided to many villages in the area from this project: the project buildings are visible from the bus. From there the road follows the River Seti through Sisuwa only 12 km from Pokhara and near the two smaller lakes of the valley. The road enters the town about halfway between the airport and the bazaar. At some points along the route, especially between Mugling and Pokhara, you can glimpse Himalchuli, Manaslu, the

Annapurnas and other peaks during the autumn and winter.

Damauli, a small town on the road between Kathmandu and Pokhara, is worth a stopover. The town's main road leads to the Panchayat building. Taking the path to the left of it will take you down to the Madi and Seti Rivers for bathing, go up stream a hundred or so yards on the right to reach a beach.

Mike Baldwin, USA

The land one sees along the route from Kathmandu to Pokhara is like a patchwork quilt – a composite of swathes of beauty from round the world. I saw rock gorge river scenes from Japanese brush paintings, hills akin to the south-west of the US as well as those from the highlands of Scotland, and the gracefully sculptured terraces, cousins to Java and Bali – consecutive changes in a day's drive.

Judy Benewitz, USA

ORIENTATION IN POKHARA

The main market or bazaar is located to the north of the bus stand while the lake area, where most visitors stay, is south. It is a long walk from the bus stop and taxis are reluctant to drive to the lake for less than Rs 10. On the other hand small taxis and minibuses shuttle between the bazaar and airport. The standard rate is Rs 2 by taxi, only Rs 1 by bus, from the airport to Mahendra Pool, located at the newer part at the beginning of the bazaar. The fare from the airport to Bagar at the far end of the bazaar is Rs 3. There are usually no buses after 5 pm. Recently the buses have started going as far as the lakeside (near the temple) and run almost every 15 minutes, so they are the most practical way of getting around in Pokhara.

Bazaar area Pokhara Bazaar consists of a two km long street, poorly planned and poorly laid out, entailing long walks to get from place to place. Most of the modern shops and the Post Office are located around Mahendra Pool. There are very few shops in the lake area. If you continue along the bazaar from Mahendra Pool and then turn left you reach Pokhara's only cinema. The campus of Pokhara's only college is also in the vicinity, while in the bazaar itself is an art gallery with paintings by Nepalese artist Durga Baral.

Airport Two of the biggest hotels in Pokhara and the tourist information are all located in this area.

Lake area Perhaps the most touristy part of Nepal, the lake area only had one or two hotels and restaurants just a decade ago. There are now more than 15 hotels with charges ranging from Rs 10 a day to over Rs 500. During the October to April season you will see hundreds of visitors camping, swimming or just sunbathing around the lake.

If you walk from the airport to the lake you come across a cluster of government buildings including the offices of the Zonal Commissioner, highest authority in the region, and the Chief of Police and Immigration. Further on you pass several trees with platforms built around them. The trees are either Banyan or Peepal and were originally planted to provide rest and shade for walkers. It was believed that such deeds resulted in a good life after death. Sometimes two trees are planted together and there is supposed to be a marriage between them.

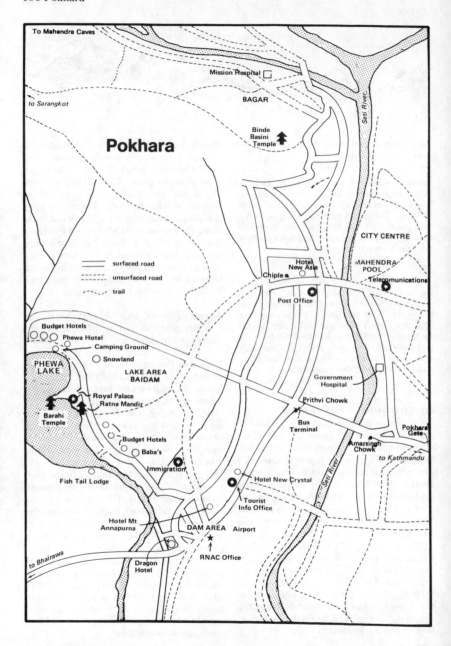

The village here is known as Baidam and its inhabitants are mainly of the Chetri caste. Due to the heavy influence of tourism here even children speak English and some have started smoking hashish. There is a new affluence and even mud huts are being rented out to the freak type travellers.

Dam Area The dam at the lake was constructed with Indian aid in the late '60s to provide electricity for Pokhara. This area, also called 'Pardi' contains a cluster of hotels run both for budget travellers and the more affluent. At this area you are still at the lake but away from the heavy lakeside tourist zone of the in Baidam. The view of the Himalayas from Pardi is much better and it is also quieter and closer to the city centre and the airport. You don't, however, have a great choice of places to eat although the hotels provide quite good food.

HOTELS & RESTAURANTS
The hotel and restaurant situation in Pokhara is changing much faster than in Kathmandu so you can expect some variations from the time this book was written. Hotels, lodges and restaurants are located in three main areas in Pokhara. Food prices are rather higher than in Kathmandu and the food is not as good.

Airport Area
Two of Pokhara's three large hotels are in this area. *Hotel New Crystal* (tel 35) has rooms ranging from US$10-15/14-25 for single/double. The *Hotel Mount Annapurna*, decorated in Tibetan style charges US$12 for a single and US$17 a double.

New Crystal Hotel – 3* – tel 36 – 34 rooms all with bath – fully air-conditioned – restaurant – bar

Hotel Mt Annapurna – 2* – tel 37 – 32 rooms with bath – restaurant – bar – roof garden

Bazaar Area
There are several cheap hotels (in the price range Rs 15 to 25) in the Mahendra Pool area. A new hotel started by Tibetan-speaking people from Menang known as *Hotel New Asia* has rooms ranging from Rs 60 to 90 a day. *Hotel Mandar* (tel 268) in the same area charges Rs 60/95 for a single/double. The bazaar area is not popular with most people as it is too far from the lake, but if you want to make an early start when trekking it may be worth overnighting there.

Lake Area
The lake area has a wide range of accommodation and most visitors stay here. For the more affluent there is the *Fish Tail Lodge* and *Dragon Hotel* while at the other end of the scale there are many lodges with single rooms in the Rs 10 to 25 range. There are also cheaper lodges and private homes, some of them just mud huts, where the impecunious and adventurous can stay for as little as Rs 5 a day. However, many people in the area recently have taken to drugs and you need to be extra careful in selecting a place to ensure that your belongings remain safe. The Lake Area can be divided into the Lakeside (east), Lakeside (west) and the Dam Area (Pardi).

Dam Area This area near the lake is liked by many because it is quieter. It has now more than seven lodges ranging from the moderately expensive *Hotel Dragon* costing US12 to cheaper ones costing less than a dollar. Many of these hotels are run by Thakalis.

The *Dragon Hotel* is the newest tourist class hotel in Pokhara and is recommended. Singles/doubles cost US$9/18 per day. As Pokhara abounds in very inexpensive hotels on the one hand and has few tourist class hotels on the other, this hotel helps to reduce the shortage of rooms in the medium class category. The owner, Hari Tulachan, is a Thakali from Kali Gandaki Valley. There are also four lodges in this

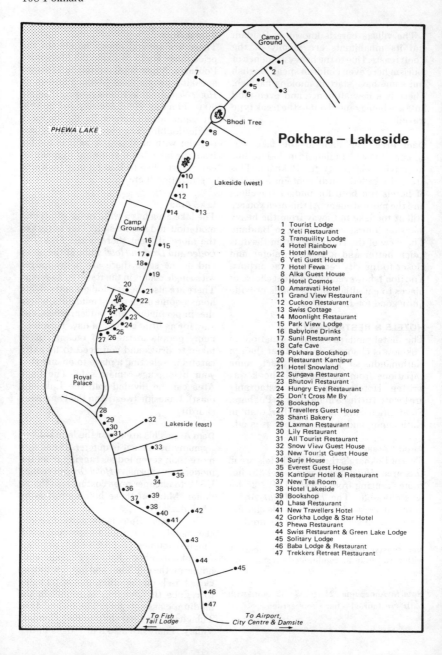

Pokhara – Lakeside

PHEWA LAKE

Bhodi Tree

Lakeside (west)

Camp Ground

Camp Ground

Royal Palace

Lakeside (east)

1 Tourist Lodge
2 Yeti Restaurant
3 Tranquility Lodge
4 Hotel Rainbow
5 Hotel Monal
6 Yeti Guest House
7 Hotel Fewa
8 Alka Guest House
9 Hotel Cosmos
10 Amaravati Hotel
11 Grand View Restaurant
12 Cuckoo Restaurant
13 Swiss Cottage
14 Moonlight Restaurant
15 Park View Lodge
16 Babylone Drinks
17 Sunil Restaurant
18 Cafe Cave
19 Pokhara Bookshop
20 Restaurant Kantipur
21 Hotel Snowland
22 Sungava Restaurant
23 Bhutovi Restaurant
24 Hungry Eye Restaurant
25 Don't Cross Me By
26 Bookshop
27 Travellers Guest House
28 Shanti Bakery
29 Laxman Restaurant
30 Lily Restaurant
31 All Tourist Restaurant
32 Snow View Guest House
33 New Tourist Guest House
34 Surje House
35 Everest Guest House
36 Kantipur Hotel & Restaurant
37 New Tea Room
38 Hotel Lakeside
39 Bookshop
40 Lhasa Restaurant
41 New Travellers Hotel
42 Gorkha Lodge & Star Hotel
43 Phewa Restaurant
44 Swiss Restaurant & Green Lake Lodge
45 Solitary Lodge
46 Baba Lodge & Restaurant
47 Trekkers Retreat Restaurant

To Fish Tail Lodge

To Airport, City Centre & Damsite

area which are run by Thakalis and are recommended. *Hotel Garden*, run by a Thakali family, has single/double for Rs 20/50 and many who stay at this hotel return. The slightly expensive *Ashok Guest House* in the same area (tel 374) has singles for Rs 85. It's located in a new building and has a nice garden. *Hotel Mount View*, also run by a Thakali family, is cheaper as singles at Rs 15 and the food is quite good. *Hotel Valley View* and *Cosmos Guest House* in the same area in a similar price range are also all right.

Next to the Hotel Garden is *Hotel Peaceful* which has some rooms with a view of the mountains and the lake – single/doubles are Rs 15/25. It is difficult to find a cheap and decent place at this price range anywhere in Pokhara.

Dragon Hotel – air conditioned – bar – restaurant 20 rooms with attached bath

Main Lake Area As there are so many new hotels and restaurants which have opened in Pokhara, the main lake area has been divided into two parts: Lakeside (east) and Lakeside (west), the dividing line being chosen arbitrarily as the vicinity of the Royal Palace. Lakeside (east) is closer to the airport and the Dam Area and was the first area of Pokhara to be developed as a tourist destination. On the other hand, Lakeside (west) was developed more recently.

Lakeside (east) The best and the most pleasant hotel in Pokhara in this area is *Fishtail Lodge*, (telex NP 2205 AAPU) named after Machhapuchhare, the peak which dominates the skyline of Pokhara. To get to the lodge, which has 23 rooms with bath, you have to cross the lake by raft. It costs US$25 for a single, US$35 a double.

From where the road branches down to the lakeside across Fishtail Lodge, a cluster of low price hotels and restaurants starts and continues beyond the lake.

Hotel Kantipur is popular with affluent budget travellers. Guests have included persons working for aid missions in Nepal and other voluntary workers. Single rooms with/without bath are US$2/8. Not all the rooms are equally good, but this is compensated to some extent by the fact that the proprietors are nice and will store your luggage for free while you go trekking. They also have special rates for long term residents.

Gurkha Lodge, five minutes away from the lake via a dirt road, is run by an ex-Gurkha soldier and his British wife. There is a beautiful garden which is like an English country garden. Prices are somewhat expensive – doubles are Rs 148. *Hotel Green Lake* is pretty basic and charges Rs 40 for a double. Many overland bus companies park their vehicles here while visiting Pokhara. *Phewa Rest House*, run by a Dutch couple, charge Rs 15/20 for a single with a common bath. *Star Lodge*, one of the cheap places, offers singles/doubles at Rs 15/25.

Lakeside (west) *Travellers Guest House* has parking and camping places and charges Rs 25/75 for single/doubles. There is a Rs 8 charge for camping. Many people who have stayed here seem to think it was worthwhile. *Hotel Fewa* is one of the few hotels which is right on the edge of the lake. Singles range from Rs 30-50, depending on attached bath. *Hotel Snowland*, long been popular with budget travellers, has been renovated and is slightly more expensive. Singles range from Rs 40 without bath to Rs 90 with. There are several new lodges which have opened beyond the boat harbour. *Alka Guest House*, run by friendly people, is in an entirely new and clean building. Singles/doubles range from Rs 25 to 150. *Hotel Monal* has double rooms ranging from Rs 75 to 125. *Yeti Guest House* has parking places and charges Rs 50/60 for a double. You may be able to bring the price down in the off season. If you're looking for rock bottom accommodation in this area, *Park Guest House* charge only Rs 24

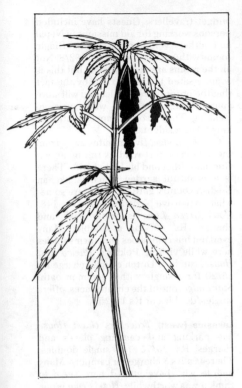

for a single and Rs 30 for a double. Also, there are so many private homes which have become 'lodges' though they often don't have names (or they change them frequently to avoid government tax).

Places to Eat in Pokhara
Pokhara does not have the variety of food available in Kathmandu. *Hotel Kantipur* in Lakeside (east) has a nice restaurant with a fireplace and has good chicken dishes. It is likely to be very crowded most of the time. *Baba Restaurant*, run by a Thakalis family, has good breakfasts. *Hungry Eyes* in Lakeside (west) has an amazing variety of pies and is definitely the best place to eat this form of cuisine in Pokhara. *Garden Hotel* and *Mountain View* in the Dam area serve inexpensive

Nepali style dal bhat tarkari dishes. The recently opened *Rodee Restaurant* in the same area serves Chinese dishes which have been recommended by some. A few travellers have also liked *Bhutovi* which serves Japanese food. *Don't Cross Me By* serves Chinese and continental dishes.

SEEING POKHARA
Although the Pokhara Valley does not have the many temples and man-made attractions of the Kathmandu Valley there is still much to see and do. Sightseeing here can be very inexpensive; some popular attractions include:

Phewa Lake The beautiful lake near Pokhara offers pleasant walking and even more pleasant boating. Small dug-out canoes can be hired near the temple in the lake. These can be rented for about Rs 5 to 10 per hour.

Rupa and Begnas Lakes The two smaller and less visited lakes in the valley are about 15 km away to the east. They're pretty, unspoilt and wild. If you enjoy trekking the walk to these lakes makes a pleasant day's outing – take a bus to the foot of the ridge which separates the two lakes and has a view of them both. The road to this place follows the Kathmandu-Pokhara road and then branches north. You can find buses leaving for Begnas at Pokhara city centre in Chiple every hour. The fare is Rs 2.75. From here a two hour walk to the trail heading north will bring you to the village of Pachabhaiyya.

Sarangkot Another pleasant day's walk will take you to the top of the hill overlooking Phewa Lake. From here you have an incredible view of the whole sweep of the Annapurna range to say nothing of the lake and Pokhara itself. It is possible to climb to Sarangkot in two hours from the lake, but the trail is not well defined. An easier route is to go to the temple of Bindebasani in the bazaar and take the trail from there to Sarangkot. The

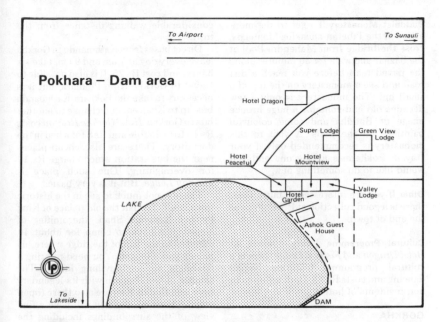

Pokhara – Dam area

To Airport

To Sunauli

Hotel Dragon

Super Lodge

Green View Lodge

Hotel Peaceful

Hotel Mountview

LAKE

Valley Lodge

Hotel Garden

Ashok Guest House

To Lakeside

DAM

path back down to the lake is easy to find and the round trip should take four to five hours.

Kahun Danda Another good view of the mountains can be had from the ridge to the east of Pokhara Bazaar known as Kahun Danda. There is a view tower there and the walk from the bazaar takes about three hours.

River Seti The river which flows through Pokhara is interesting in that it often disappears underground. At some places the milky coloured water, due to the limestone in the soil, flows as much as 50 metres below the surface. Pokhara's often heavy rainfall does not lie on the ground but tends to be soaked up immediately. The bridge near the Mission Hospital at the end of the bazaar offers the best view of the Seti River.

Mahendra Gufa These limestone caves have been ransacked by souvenir hunters

leaving little to see, but the walk there is very pleasant. The trail to the caves crosses the bridge at Bagar at the end of the bazaar and heads toward the village of Batulechaur. The walk to the caves takes about two hours. Batulechaur used to be well known for its oranges, but a virus epidemic destroyed all the trees in the valley and Pokhara, once renowned for excellent oranges and tangerines must now import them.

Tibetan Refugee Camp The refugee camp at the village of Hengja is about four hours' walk from the airport, a couple of hours shorter if you start out from Bagar at the end of the town. There are many handicrafts for sale and you can see how this colony of displaced persons has now become self-sufficient with the aid of Swiss training. There are smaller workshops near the lake. You can reach one by following the river downstream.

Buddhist Monastery To get to the monastery of the Tibetan-speaking Mannagis, cross the bridge from Mahendra Pool at the bazaar and walk for 30 minutes along the paved road before you reach a dirt road and see a monastery on the top of a small hill. The monastery is only a few decades old and contains a huge bronze image of Buddha and some colourful paintings on the walls. A visit to this monastery is recommended only if your stay in Pokhara is a long one and you would like to do something new.

Other If you are interested in butterflies, there is a good collection at PN College at the end of town.

Cultural Programme Every evening at *Hotel Dragon* and *Fishtail Lodge* there is a cultural programme featuring Nepali dancing and costs Rs 35. Both are open to non-residents of hotels.

GORKHA

Gorkha – the ancient capital of the principality of Gorkha that gave the feared Gurkha soldiers their name and from which King Prithvi Narayan Shah set out to unify all of Nepal – is approximately halfway between Pokhara and Kathmandu. Trekkers walking between the two towns on the more southerly route can pass through Gorkha or it can be reached on foot from the Pokhara-Kathmandu highway. The airstrip called Gorkha is actually a considerable walking distance from the town.

Direct buses from Kathmandu to Gorkha leave every day at 7 am and 9 am, take six hours, and cost Rs 25. It is also possible to travel to Gorkha from Pokhara, but it is necessary to take the Pokhara-Kathmandu bus up to Khaireni and change to another bus to Gorkha. *Hotel Gorkha Bisauni* costs Rs 40 for a double and Rs 8 for a bed in the dormitory. There are also cheap places near the bus station which charge Rs 10 for overnighting. One such place is *Thakali Lodge*. But it is very basic.

There is not much to see in the historic town itself. To visit the old palace of King Prithvi Narayan Shah, the unifier of Nepal, you have to climb for about 40 minutes to the top of the ridge where his palace was situated. You need to bring a flashlight to see anything inside. The temple of Gorkhanath with its legendary cave and that of Kali are also there (open only to Hindus) and you will have a fine view of the surroundings including the Annapurna and Himalchuli ranges.

Two centuries ago, when Nepal consisted of many small kingdoms in the hills, the palaces were always constructed on hill tops. After your visit here you will realise the difficulties the ruler of such a small kingdom faced when setting out to defeat the Malla kings of the fertile Kathmandu Valley, and in starting the unification of a country more than a hundred times it size.

Pokhara
Top: Rural home near Pokhara
Bottom: Machhapuchhare from the Bindebasini Temple in Pokhara

The Himalaya
Top: Namche Bazar in the Solu Kumbhu
Left: On the trail from Namche to Tyangboche
Right: Tyangboche Monastery and Ama Dablam

The Himalaya

THE MOUNTAINS

The main peaks in the Nepal Himalaya, from east to west, are:

Peak	Height	First Ascent
Kanchenjunga	8598	1955 British
Makalu	8475	1955 French
Lhotse	8501	1955 Swiss
Everest	8848	1953 British
Muptse	7906	1961 British
Cho Oyu	8153	1954 Australian

visible from Kathmandu

Peak	Height	First Ascent
Gauri Shankar	7145	
Phurbi Ghyachu	5722	
Dorje Lakpa	6975	
Langtang	7246	1959 Japanese
Ganesh Himal	7406	1955 Franco-Swiss
Himalchuli	7892	1960 Japanese
Manaslu	7850	1956 Japanese

visible from Pokhara

Peak	Height	First Ascent
Annapurna	8090	1950 French
Annapurna 2	7937	1960 British, Indo-Nepal
Annapurna 3	7502	1961 Indian
Annapurna 4	7525	1955 German
Machhapuchhare	7059	
Dhaulagiri	8137	1960 Swiss

Nepal has the highest peak in the world – Mt Everest – and six others over 8000 metres, and it was mountain climbers attempting to conquer the 'top of the world' who were amongst the first 'tourists' to enter Nepal. Most of the major peaks were climbed in the fifties and sixties but Himalayan mountaineering has lost none of its appeal.

While trekking you are unlikely to go above 3500 metres unless you are walking to the Everest base camp, but breathtaking views are easily found. Mt Everest is not visible from the Kathmandu Valley, but from Nagarkot on top of the ridge to the eastern end of the valley you can pick it out in the distance. The view here extends from the extreme east of Nepal to Dhaulagiri in the west. Dhulikhel also provides a fine Himalayan panorama although Everest is not so clearly visible. Kakani, to the north-west of Kathmandu, provides a good view of the western Himalayas, particularly Ganesh Himal. A very fine view can be had from Daman on the road to the Indian border – a mountain profile to help you identify the peaks from Nagarkot or Daman can be obtained from the tourist information offices. If your stay in Kathmandu permits, visits to Sheopuri to the north and Phulchoki to the south are also worthwhile.

A number of peaks are clearly visible from Kathmandu particularly Ganesh Himal; its three peaks are seen slightly to the north-west. The lesser peaks of Dorje Lakpa (6975 metres) and Chobha Bhamare (5970 metres) almost dominate the Kathmandu skyline. East of Ganesh Himal the snow-covered peak of Langtang can be seen partially hidden by closer mountains. East of Dorje Lakpa the massive block descending slowly to the east is Phurbi Ghyachu. Further to the east no major peaks are visible until the massive bulk of Gauri Shankar, which can only be seen from the north-east of the valley.

The view from Pokhara is much better than from Kathmandu, and a walk up to Sarangkot is worthwhile for the startling span of the Annapurnas with the perfectly symmetrical shape of Machhapuchhare standing before them. If you are trekking north-west, a trip to Pun Hill, just above Ghodepani, will provide an incredible sight. Machhapuchhare gets its unusual name, the 'fish tail' mountain, from its split appearance when viewed from the east – it is still a 'virgin', unclimbed, peak. In Nepali, Annapurna means 'full of grain' and this long series of ridges does indeed look like the result of a recent harvest.

On the Jomosom trek the view from Pun Hill (near Ghodepani) on a clear morning is the most beautiful sight I have seen anywhere in the world. If it is cloudy at Ghodepani it is worth waiting for as long as it takes to clear.

R McArthur, England

MOUNTAINEERING

The sport of mountaineering came into vogue in Europe during the Victorian era and once the major Alpine peaks had been conquered European mountaineers naturally turned their eyes to the greater challenge of the Himalaya. The natural difficulties in climbing these far higher mountains were compounded, during the 1920s and 1930s, by the continued seclusion of Nepal. Expeditions were chiefly launched from the Tibetan side of the range and, attempting the major prize first, were mainly on Everest.

In 1921, 1922 and 1924 a series of British attempts on the world's high peak resulted in a maximum height attained at 8572 metres, just 300 metres short of the summit. This height was actually reached in 1924 without the use of oxygen although the earlier 1922 expedition had used it to reach 8326 metres. Already the pattern for future expeditions with their large contingent of porters had been set – the 1924 expedition used 350.

In 1925 the British climbers Mallory, who coined the famous mountaineer's explanation 'because it's there', and Irvine disappeared in an attempt that may have actually reached the summit – their bodies were never found. A series of less successful attempts followed through the 1930s although several did succeed in climbing to beyond 8000 metres. A strange solo attempt in 1934 by Maurice Wilson added another name to those climbers who lost their lives on Everest.

After the war the greater affluence in the west, improved equipment, skills and oxygen apparatus together with the re-opening of Nepal, led to a series of new assaults both on Everest and other peaks. In 1951 a reconnaissance expedition included amongst its numbers the New Zealand climber Edmund Hillary and a Swiss expedition in 1952 sent Sherpa climber Norgay Tensing to 7500 metres. Finally in 1953 John Hunt's British team succeeded in getting Tensing and Hillary to the highest spot on earth.

Once conquered, success on Everest followed repeatedly. A Swiss expedition reached the top in 1956 and in 1960 it was the turn of a party from the People's Republic of China. Members of the massive American expedition in 1963, nearly a thousand climbers and porters, found the Chinese flag on top. An Indian expedition reached the summit in 1965 and in 1970 a Japanese team not only reached the top but sent one fearless climber back down on skis! Several more attempts included a successful Italian team in 1973 and the International Women's Year victory of the Japanese women's party.

Other Himalayan peaks had also been comprehensively attacked in the fifties and sixties. The successful French expedition under Maurice Herzog on Annapurna in 1950 in 1950 was probably the best known, for not only was this the first peak over 8000 metres to 'fall', but the mountain fought back, forcing the climbers to descend from the summit in appalling weather. Badly frostbitten, Herzog and his partner paid dearly for their challenge in fingers and toes. While the large expeditions successfully reached the top of one major peak after another, a new breed of up and coming climbers were cutting their teeth on Alpine and North American peaks. Eschewing the 'easy' ridge routes they went for the most difficult faces, attacking them with carefully developed skills and high technology, space age equipment. Chris Bonnington exemplified this trend in his 1970 climb on the south face of Annapurna and following this up with a skillfully orchestrated rush to the top of Everest by the 'impossible' south-west face in 1975.

Mountain climbing is now looked upon

by the government of Nepal as a useful source of income as well as a generator of publicity. A royalty has to be paid for each attempt – the higher the peak the greater the fee. Detailed applications have to be made and at present Everest is fully 'booked' for years to come. Until recently only one expedition was allowed on any given peak in each season – the post-monsoon and pre-monsoon parts of the dry season. This rule has now been relaxed and more than one party can climb at once. The Chinese are also allowing attempts on Everest from their side of the border. The Nepalese Government has also started approving winter expeditions to Everest recently. Teams booked on Everest during the late 1980s include French, Japanese, British, French, Italian,

Korean, Spanish, Yugoslavian, West German, American, Indian, Polish and New Zealand teams.

There are still many major peaks which have not been successfully climbed, some not even attempted. But some observers hope the next wave of activity may be a retreat from the massive, costly, high technology expeditions to a smaller, more manageable scale. Kathmandu's trekking shops have so much high quality equipment gleaned from the left-overs of major expeditions that a small party could be equipped right there. The 1978 Austrian expedition to Everest that put Reinhold Messner and Peter Habler on top without the use of oxygen may be a pointer in that direction.

Trekking

Trekking – hiking along the trails that form the main links between Nepal's isolated villages and settlements – is one of the country's main attractions. Almost unheard of until the last decade, trekking is now for many visitors the only reason they come to Nepal at all.

WHY TREK?
A trek in Nepal is a unique and unforgettable experience for a whole range of reasons, but four in particular stand out:

Scenery Eight of the 10 highest mountains in the world are in Nepal and if you want to see them from close up you must walk. While trekking you'll see far more than mountains – you can walk from tropical lowlands to alpine meadows and glacial moraines, while in the spring Nepal's brilliant rhododendrons will be in bloom and you may see rare species of birds.

Safety Not only is the scenery interesting and ever changing but it can be seen in relative safety. Theft, robbery, assault – all the problems of western civilisation and many Asian countries – are relatively unknown in Nepal. There was a time a few years ago when even women could trek alone in Nepal. Unfortunately, things seem to be changing and trekkers need to be more careful than they used to be. It is advisable to trek in groups of at least two persons and if possible with a porter or guide. But this does not necessarily mean that you need to trek with an organised trekking agency in an expensive way.

Diversity Nepal is a country of contrasts and this extends to the people as well as the landscape. Trekkers pass through picturesque villages inhabited by Sherpas, Gurungs, Magars, Newars, Brahmins, Tamangs and many other ethnic groups who co-exist in Nepal.

People Trekkers are always impressed by the friendliness of the people they meet along the local trails, which are in constant use and humming with activity. This is a totally different experience from hiking along the often uninhabited trails in the US Rockies, European Alps or Australian bushland. Above all, no household in a village would turn away a weary traveller arriving late in the evening – there are frequent possibilities of staying in Nepali homes.

ON THE TRAIL
A trek can last half a day or for over a month. A short walk up to Nagarkot to see the sunrise only takes three hours while the walk to the Everest Base Camp will take at least three weeks. Make sure you enjoy walking before setting out on a long trek.

Height Trekking is not mountaineering but it is as well to remember that the Himalayas begin where other mountains finish. An average trek oscillates between 1000 metres and 3000 metres but the trek to the Everest Base Camp will reach 5545 metres. Most of the time you will remain within the altitude range 1500 metres to 2000 metres. It is important to remember that 4000 metres in Nepal is not the same as in Europe or North America as the country is much closer to the equator.

A Day on the Trail Trekking usually consists of a series of ascents or descents, walking five or six hours in the day. To ensure good acclimatisation at high altitudes it is wise to halt for the night at a lower level than the high point reached during the day. A long midday meal stop is usually made and the night can be spent in a village tea shop or in camp – depending on whether you are on your own or with an organised trekking company.

When to Trek The best trekking season is in October and November just after the monsoon – visibility will be clear and the weather mild. March is the next best season and has the added bonus of the rhododendrons and other flowers. Trekking can be done and enjoyed in December, January and February but it can get very cold – particularly at night. April and May are good months for doing high altitude treks, but trekking is not possible between June and September when the monsoon rains make the trails extremely slippery and the leeches come out to make walking miserable. Some people do trek in early June and late September.

Where to Stay If you are trekking independently you stay either in tea houses or in private homes in villages. If you are with an organised trekking group everything is taken care of and you will sleep mainly in tents set up by the porters. Some tea stalls and homes have started making a small charge, Rs 1 to 5, for an overnight stay but usually accommodation is free, providing you take the evening meal there. If you go by yourself to an uninhabited area you may have to sleep in a cave or an abandoned building.

PRELIMINARIES

Trekking Permits Every trekker must carry a trekking permit when away from the areas permitted in the visa. No trekking permits are, however, needed for walking in the Kathmandu or Pokhara Valley or along short treks such as Dhulikhel and Namobuddha. Trekking permits are issued for one destination at a time along proscribed routes. They cost Rs 60 per week initially and Rs 75 per week for the second month. The permits can be obtained in Kathmandu and in Pokhara.

Equipment If you do not already have good equipment it can be bought or rented from one of the trekking shops. The equipment is often top quality but although daily

Sherpa

rental charges are reasonable a large deposit may be required – a good down-filled sleeping bag, a rucksack, down pants and down jacket can each be rented for around Rs 7 per day, but the total deposit can easily come to over US$100. It is advisable to have your own strong, comfortable boots – they can be rented but people with large feet may have trouble finding suitable footwear. If a rented sleeping bag does not look perfectly clean have it dry cleaned. *Himal Hiking Home* in Yetkha, one block from Durbar Square and *Annapurna Mountaineering & Trekking* in Thamel have a wide range of gear. You can also find items in Freak Street and equipment can be rented in Pokhara too.

POPULAR TREKS

Trek	Location	Time	From – To
Everest	to Solu Khumbu region of east Nepal	1 to 5 weeks	Bus to Jiri or fly to Lukla then walk to the base camp
Langtang	North to Kathmandu	12 days	Bus to Trisulu then walk to the Langtang Valley
Helambu	North of Kathmandu	7 days	Bus to Panchka or go via Sundarijal
Kathmandu-Sheopuri	Highest point on the hill north of Kathmandu	8 hours	Walk from Budhanilkantha and return via Sundarijal
Kathmandu-Nagarkot	Hilltop north-east of Kathmandu	3 hours	Bus to Bhaktapur then walk
Dhulikhel-Namobuddha	East of Kathmandu Valley	1 day	Bus to Dhulikhel then walk
Annapurna Sanctuary	North of Pokhara	12 days	Walk from Pokhara via Naudanda, Birethanti and Ghandruk
Ghandruk-Ghodepani	North of Pokhara	7 days	Walk from Pokhara to Ghandruk
Pokhara-Jomosom-Muktinath	North-west of Pokhara	12 days	Routes via Birethanti or via Kusma and Beni
Manang	North-east of Pokhara	2 weeks	Dumre to Manang
Pokhara-Sarangkot	North of Pokhara	1 day	Walk from Bindebasini temple in Pokhara bazaar

Incidentals The food available along the trail is normally limited in its variety so bring along some cheese, dried fruit and canned food. It will be almost impossible to change money along the way so carry adequate Nepali currency in small denominations. Take cigarettes and matches, they are widely appreciated small gifts. Please don't spoil the children who in some regions come up asking for 'one rupee'. A torch (flashlight) is indispensable for late night trips to the outhouses and matches or salt for getting rid of leeches if you trek in the wet.

Health Medical care along the trail is almost non-existent except for the Edmund Hillary Hospital at Khumjung in the Solu Khumbu, so make sure that you are fit and healthy before departing. A rescue helicopter is extremely expensive! Take care of yourself along the trail by ensuring that

Maximum height	Interesting Sights	Comments
Tyangboche – 3875 metres, Kala Patar – 5545 metres	Walk through interesting Sherpa villages to stunning views of Everest, Ama Dablam, Nuptse, Lhotse	very touristy from Lukla on
4200 metres	Pass through ethnically Tibetan villages like Tamang, en route to the glacier at the foot of Langtang peak	stay in lodges along trail
Tarkeghyang – 2800 metres	Friendly people and chances to stay in Sherpa homes but poor views of the peaks	
2700 metres	Walk through forests with excellent mountain views, can overnight in a tent	
2000 metres	Good scenery including Everest, can overnight in a lodge	
1700 metres	Pleasant one-day walk along a typical trail to an old stupa marking a legendary spot	
3275 metres	Pass through Gurung villages en route to the foot of Annapurna, excellent views	2 days through uninhabited areas
2700 metres	Excellent views of Annapurna and Machhapuchhare en route to village of Ghandruk	
2700 metres	Most interest trek Nepal, cross the Himalayan range between Annapurna and Dhaulagiri	
3600 metres	Valley north of Annapurna Range inhabited by Tibetan-speaking people known as Manangs	Only open since 1976, can reach Muktinath by 5600-metre pass
1700 metres	Excellent views of Annapurna and the Pokhara Valley, see ruins of a 17th-century fort	

water is boiled – remember that fresh tea is always safe. Diarrhoea can be the curse of trekkers so bring appropriate medication. A high altitudes almost everyone suffers from headaches so aspirin is advisable as are sleeping tablets to ensure good sleep. Sunburn can also be a problem at altitude, a barrier cream will protect your skin and good sunglasses are necessary for you eyes. Blisters are another problem so a supply of band-aids is advisable.

The most serious health problem the unwary trekker can fall prey to is the dreaded mountain sickness – this is a major, even deadly, danger for the careless or foolhardy trekker. Mountain sickness is a form of pulmonary oedema and usually hits young and healthy people who do not heed the warnings and go 'too high, too fast'. Prevention is simple – take things easy and ensure plenty of acclimatisation. The first signs often show themselves at night and this is why it is best to sleep at a lower altitude than the maximum reached during the day. The mild symptoms are low urine output, bad headaches, sleeplessness and lots of appetite, followed in extreme cases by nausea, vomiting, severe fatigue, mental confusion, breathlessness and apathy. If you get mountain sickness there's just one answer – get down to a lower altitude as quickly and with as little effort as possible.

Maps The series of *Mandala* trekking maps are readily available in shops in Kathmandu. They include Kathmandu to Pokhara, Pokhara to Jomosom, Jomosom to Jumla and Surkhet, Lamosangu to Mt Everest and Helambu-Langtang. All have a useful glossary of Nepali words and walking times along the trails.

ARRANGEMENTS

Independent trekking Most of the young people visiting Nepal trek independently. While the organised treks have all arrangements made by the trekking agency, including porters and food, independent travellers carry their own luggage (or just hire a porter), spend overnight at tea stalls, lodges and sometimes private homes along the way and eat local food. Although not much English is spoken in the villages along most of the trekking routes, it is becoming more easily understood. There are more than 30 trekking agencies in Nepal. The larger and better established of them are more interested in bigger groups. Smaller agencies are more interested in independent trekkers. There are actually two trekking agencies that specialise in low cost trekking. *Sherpa Trekking Services*, Kamaladi (tel 2012489) will help you organise your trek at a minimum cost. It can also arrange the services of an English-speaking guide or rent trekking equipment. If you are interested in joining an organised group with this agency it will cost you in the range of US$20-37 a day depending upon the facilities you need. If you just want to

hire guides, it can provide them at about Rs 60 a day.

Great Himalayan Adventure (tel 2-16144) can arrange treks in the US$22-28 range. It caters mainly to the French market. During the off-season, you can also just hire porters and guides for as low as US$5 a day.

Independent trekking is much easier with the services of a porter who can be hired for Rs 30 to Rs 40 per day. This aid to easy trekking is particularly invaluable at high altitudes where just getting up the ascents will be quite sufficient for most people. When agreeing a price with a porter make sure whether or not you are paying for the porter's meals. In the hills, porters can easily be found at most villages or at the airfields where there will usually be a few who have just despatched a group back to Kathmandu. Porters do not often speak English but will help you find overnight accommodation as well as carry the load and act as a guide. The most popular area for independent trekkers is around Pokhara, possibly because it is easy to find food and lodging there.

Organised Trekking Several trekking companies in Nepal will arrange sleeping bags, porters, tents, food and also experienced English speaking Sherpa guides. All you need to carry is your own clothes and camera. Trek charges vary from US$20 to US$80 per day depending on the number of people in the group and the duration of the trek. One of the better known trekking organizations in Nepal is *Mountain Travels* (PO Box 170, tel 4-14508) whose well known manager Col. J O M Roberts has organized many mountaineering expeditions. Another well known company is *Himalayan Journeys* on Kantipath whose American manager is the author of 'Trekking in the Himalayas'. In the US tours can be booked through Mountain Travel, 1398 Folano Ave., Albany, California 94706. In England, Mountain Travel treks can be booked through Thomas Cook, London.

ROYAL NEPAL AIRLINES

yeti
SERVICE

Annapurna Mountaineering & Trekking on Durbar Marg is also well known and charges between US$30 to $40 per day. *Sherpa Co-operatives* (tel 2-15887) likes to call itself a 'quality oriented organization' and charges between US$30-40 per day. Some of its treks are to non-touristy and unusual destinations. *Great Himalayan Adventure* (tel 2-16144) has organized French expeditions and caters for French groups. *Lama Excursions* in Durbar Marg (tel 2-15840) charges between US$20-35 a day and is popular with affluent budget travellers.

Ausventure is a very well known and respected name for organising treks from Australia. Its address is PO Box 54, Mosman, NSW 2088. *Australian Himalayan Expeditions*, 28-34 O'Connel St, Sydney, NSW 2000 also brings a large number of Australians to Nepal. Many British trekkers organise their treks through *Sherpa Expeditions*, 3 Bedford Rd, London W4.

All the organised trekking companies require plenty of notice to fix up a trek. Try to allow at least two months.

The Yeti
No description of Nepal can be complete without a mention of the famous Yeti – the abominable snowman. This mysterious, ape-like creature lives high in the remotest regions of the Himalayas and has been talked and written about; feared by the hill people; searched for by westerners; 'seen' by countless people – but never photographed. Footprints in the snow are the only trace the shy yeti likes to leave, but these are often thought to be normal size human prints that have grown as the sun melted the snow around them. Similarly the yeti scalps in the Solu Khumbu region, in particularly the one at the Pangboche monastery, have all turned out to be fakes. Despite the scientific reluctance to accept the yeti's existence everyone would like to believe in it – so keep your camera handy when trekking.

TREKS
There are countless different routes and treks around Nepal. The following are just a few of the most popular 'standard' routes.

EVEREST TREK
The trek to the base camp at the foot of Mt Everest takes three weeks at a minimum. This is not as easy as trekking in the Pokhara area as the trail traverses regions which have remained relatively backward and closed to outside influences. The Sherpa country in the vicinity of Everest is an exception, of course, since there have been so many mountaineering expeditions in this area in the past 25 years.

The usual starting point for the trek is Jiri which is connected to Lamosangu on the road to the Chinese border but if time is limited the trek can be shortened by flying between Kathmandu and Lukla, only a few days walk from the base camp. If you only intend to fly one way it is best to go back from Lukla as this gives greater acclimatisation to the altitude. If you fly directly from Kathmandu at 1300 metres to Lukla at 2800 metres, and then start climbing to the base camp at 5340 metres, great care must be taken to acclimatise yourself sufficiently. Flights to Lukla are now on a regular basis, but at the height of the trekking season, although departures are frequent, cloudy weather can easily shut the hill country STOL fields for several days at a time. Per person cost is about US$55.

The Everest trek is relatively rough as you have many ascents and descents to make. Between Jiri and Surkya near Lukla the trail repeatedly climbs over mountain passes as high as 3500 metres and then descends to valleys, as low as 1000 metres, while crossing the rivers that run from the north. There are occasional bazaars and market places along the way. From Surkya at 2343 metres to Namche Bazaar, 3440 metres, and then to the base camp it us an almost continuous ascent. It has been estimated that the trek from Lamosangu to the base camp – taking into account the total number of ascents and descents – approaches twice the height of Everest!

On the way you pass through villages inhabited by Tamangs, Sunuwars, Rais and, finally, Sherpas plus some Brahmin-Chetri villages and occasional Newari ones, mainly the bazaars. In other words you walk from the Nepali speaking, Hindu lowlands to the mongoloid, Tibetan-Buddhist highlands with many opportunities to observe Nepal's rich ethnic mix. The most interesting area to visit in the Everest trek is the Sherpa country after you reach Changma or Junibesi walking from Lamosangu, or Lukla if you fly in from Kathmandu. According to the finding of a well-known British anthropologist, no other Tibetan speaking people in Nepal can be compared with the Sherpas 'in the high standard of living, spirit of enterprise, sense of civic responsibility, social polish and general devotion to the practice of

Hill ambulance service

Buddhism'. Actually, the 'Sherpa Country' is also the safest area in Nepal to trek. Unlike other trails where thefts are beginning to appear, this does not seem to have become a problem here. A portion of the road from Lamosangu to Jiri has now been completed and it is possible to start the trek in Jiri.

The main crop of the Khumbu region is potato. Although the economy of Sherpa villages used to depend solely on potato cultivation – itself a recent introduction – tourism is becoming increasingly important. New Zealand has helped Nepal in setting up the Everest National Park which is in the catchment area of the Dudh Kosi and Imja rivers. Under the project, attempts are made to conserve forest, landscape and wildlife in the area, provide facilities for visitors and raise the standard of living of the local people.

Kathmandu to Jiri

There are buses leaving for Jiri in the morning and the trip lasts the whole day.

Jiri

It's worthwhile spending a full day and night in the beautiful valley of Jiri. The valley was developed with Swiss assistance in the 1960s and has a STOL field and hospital. It costs US$31 to fly from Kathmandu directly to Jiri and start your trek from there. The weekly market, or 'hat', is held on Saturdays and well worth seeing.

Day 1: Jiri-Thodung (eight hours walking)
The fair-sized Newar town of Those is only a few hours walk from Jiri. It used to be famous for the extraction of iron ore and the manufacture of khukris. This is a good place to buy supplies and in spring, summer or autumn a trip to the Thodung cheese factory is a must. Thodung at 3091 metres is only two hours from the main trail and you can buy yak cheese and other luxuries. On the way you pass through Changma (2040 metres), the first of many Sherpa villages with typical mani walls.

Do not miss stopping at the Thodung Cheese Factory for great cheese omelettes, fine hospitality and a cup of coffee that is out of this world. It is only an hour away from the main trail.

Robert Hanchett, USA

Day 2: Thodung-Sete (six hours walking)
A 500 metre descent brings you to the Likhu Khola River followed by a 2000 metre ascent to the Lamjura Pass at 3530 metres. That would be too much for one day so it is best to stop at the village of Sete (3575 metres), still a thousand metre climb from the river.

Day 3: Sete-Junibesi (six hours walking)
The Lamjura Pass will reward you with rhododendron flowers in spring and snow in winter. From the top it is a thousand metre descent to the village of Junibesi at

2675 metres. It is very popular with most visitors and there is a beautiful monastery, supposed to be the oldest in the Solu Khumbu area, just an hour away from the main trail. A good view of Numbur peak can be seen from the village.

Day 4:Junibesi-Manidingma (six hours walking)
A 700-metre ascent takes you to the Salung Ridge, then a 500-metre descent follows to the Solu Khola River. The beautiful village of Ringmo, with apple orchards, is just three hours from Junibesi and is followed by another climb to the Taksindu Pass at 3200 metres. There is a monastery with a guest house and cheese factory nearby and the view from the pass includes the mountains and .the Dudh Kosi River. A descent follows to the village of Manidingma at 2316 metres.

Day 5 & 6: Manidingma-Kharekhola-Kharte
The Dudh Kosi River is an 800 metre descent from Manidingma. The river carries water melted from Everest itself. It is a climb once more up to the village of Kharekhola (2073 metres) and then the village of Puiyan (2835 metres). Lukla, with its STOL field, is slightly off the main trail and higher up. It is situated on a 'terrace' at an altitude of 3000 metres. It also contains a modern Sherpa hotel where singles cost US$10 and up, while a more reasonably priced STS charges Rs 5 in the dormitory.

Day 7: Lukla-Ghat-Namche Bazaar (eight hours walking)
From this point it is almost all up into the Sherpa country. You descend to the Dudh Kosi River and follow it, crossing it twice up to Jorsale, the official entrance to the park (Rs 60 entry fee). Before Jorsale there is a pleasant hotel at Manjo, site of a vegetable farm for the Everest View there is a pleasant hotel at Manjo, once the site of a vegetable farm for the Everest View Hotel. You could get a good quality green salad at this place!

Namche, at 3440 metres, is the 'Sherpa capital', and the best known of the Sherpa villages because of the many Sherpas from around here who go on mountaineering expeditions. It is also the centre of the handicrafts industry and the place where trekking permits may be checked. Saturday is the market day in Namche. The village of Kunde, near Namche, has a hospital built with New Zealand aid. A mica plant is being set up in Namche with Austrian assistance.

The *International Footrest* is a good place to stay in Namche. Higher up the hill the very expensive Japanese-owned *Everest* The hotel has had a rather chequered history and closing down the Namche Bazar airstrip – RNAC no longer has aircraft suitable to fly there – resulted in its closure. When it was open rooms cost US$100+ per night – still, you could view Everest from your bathtub at this place!

Day 8: Namche-Tyangboche (five hours walking)

The Tyangboche STOL field is a short climb above Namche but is not currently in use. Slightly higher than this is the *Everest View Hotel* and from here the trail descends to meet the main Namche-Tyangboche trail and continues down to the Dudh Kosi where there is a small tea shop and a series of picturesque water-driven prayer wheels. A steep ascent brings you to the famous monastery of Tyangboche (3875 metres). The monastery is totally surrounded by mountain peaks and offers a fine view of Everest and Ama Dablam. On the full moon night of the month of November the colourful Mani Rimdu festival is held here with much singing and dancing.

The most scenic part of the Everest trek is between Tyangboche and Pangboche and it is at this altitude where the good points of trekking can really be appreciated.

Phil Martin, England

Day 9 & 10: Thyangboche-Pheriche-Lobuche

Beyond Tyangboche it is important to ensure that you are in good physical shape. A descent and ascent takes you to Pangboche where the monastery has a 'yeti scalp'. Pheriche is the last Sherpa village and has a first aid post, where there is usually a doctor. It also offers an excellent view of Everest. There are tea shops at Lobuche (4930 metres) but little shelter is available beyond this point and unless you are on an organised trek with tents it is best to use Lobuche as a base and make day treks from here. Kala Pathar (5545 metres) offers the best view of Everest obtainable anywhere. The mountain is not actually visible from the base camp (5340 metres) but it's still worth visiting, as is the lake at Gorak Shep (5160 metres).

Important Note The number of days given here is the minimum number of walking days. It is important to be adequately rested and acclimatised, and a day's rest at Namche and Tyangboche is particularly advisable. Remember that the victims of altitude sickness are often the fittest and healthiest people who foolishly over-extend themselves.

If you have walked all the way from Lamosangu you may like to consider extending the trek by walking south to Katari in the Terai, via Salleri, a four-day walk. It is especially pleasant in the winter and is still not frequented by many western trekkers. From Katari you can take a bus to Kathmandu or to Darjeeling via the East-West Highway.

HELAMBU TREK

If your time is limited and you cannot go far from the Kathmandu Valley the Helambu trek takes you to a Sherpa area where you can see how these fine Buddhist people differ from their lowland neighbours. The trek lasts a week or 10 days and does not fo above 3000 metres.

The two main villages of Helambu,

Tarkeghyang and Sermathan, are situated at 2800 metres and 2600 metres respectively so you are not in really high country. It is possible to climb higher to the Gosainkund lake (4290 metres) or go to the Langtang Valley through the Ganja La Pass (5106 metres), but this high altitude pass is only feasible between May and September. Spectacular views of the Himalayan peaks are only to be found if you go higher on this trek. But as compensation the people are friendly and hospitable and almost every Sherpa house in the region will be quickly converted to 'hotel' to welcome tourists as 'paying guests'.

During the Rana period the Helambu region was well known for its beautiful Sherpa girls many of whom worked for aristocratic Rana families in Kathmandu. The area has, therefore, been open to outside influence for a long time and almost everybody understands Nepali. Recently many people have gone to work on road construction in north-east India but almost all of them come back during February-March. In the summer most of the people left in the villages are either very young or very old.

In the Tibetan language the word for Helambu means both radish and potato, and the area is heavily dependent economically on both these products. Rice and wheat cannot be grown at this altitude. Large quantities of radishes and potatoes are exported to the lowlands in exchange for rice and other commodities. Apples are also grown in the Helambu area.

Helambu is a region, not a specific village. There are two ways to get to Helambu from Kathmandu and it is probably best to go one way and return the other. From Panchkal on the road to the Chinese border you can follow the Melemchi River to Tarkeghyang, the most important village in the region. This route also involves only two days of uphill walking whereas the alternate route from Sundarijal requires an ascent followed by

two days of descent, before more uphill work. The Sundarijal route offers a good view of the mountains from Patibhanjyang, and both routes meet in the village of Taran Maran before the steepest ascent. Sundarijal, at the northern end of the Kathmandu Valley, can be reached by taxi or you can bus to Bodhnath and walk there in three hours.

Trek to Helambu to see Sherpa houses, wood carved cabinets and fantastic brass and copper pots. The people will serve you rice, dal and Sherpa tea consisting of tea, ghee and salt.

Udi Grothelaw, Australia

Day 1: Panchkal-Bahunpati (seven hours walking)
An early start from Kathmandu is essential to reach Bahunpati on the first day. The 6 am bus will get you to Panchkal by 9 am. The trail follows the Indrawati River and involves no steep ascents or descents. Bahunpati is a small bazaar and has some government offices and a recently constructed tourist bungalow.

Day 2: Bahunpati-Taran Maran (four hours walking)
You continue to follow the Indrawati River to the village of Melemchi (820 metres) from where the trail follows the Melemchi River to Taran Maran at 1204 metres. The Sundarijal Trail joins this one here. There are also a number of places to stay here, and the short walk allows plenty of rest before the steep climb the next day.

Day 3: Taran Maran-Tarkeghyang
If you are a good walker you may be able to reach Tarkeghyang the same evening you start from Taran Maran. As it is a climb of almost 1800 metres to the village you may not make it and may have to stop in Kiul at 1500 metres, Thimpu at 1680 metres, or Kakani at 1850 metres.

The trek to Helambu offers alternative routes of three to four days and friendly homes for overnight stays along most of the way. Individual farms and homes are preferable especially in Tarkeghyang which has a landing pad for helicopter tourists and a noticeably higher standard of living.

Ron Bitzer, USA

Day 4: Tarkeghyang-Sermathan (four hours walking)

A French student once told me that Tarkeghyang resembled a village in the alps. You'll reach it on the fourth day if not before. There is a festival in the village on the full moon in March with a feast in the evening and a masked dance, which goes o till midnight. The ceremony takes place in a new monastery. The houses are clustered together in Tarkeghyang in contrast to the next village of Sermathan, only three to four hours' walk away with no steep ascents or descents. Sermathan is at an altitude of 2600 metres and the trail runs through a beautiful forest. Less commercialised than Tarkeghyang, Sermathan is also an important apple growing area and has a government horticulture farm. Although the mountains visible are not particularly notable the view is scenic and the beautiful natural setting also gives a good view of the valley of the Melemchi river to the south.

Day 5: Sermathan-Taran Maran

On your way back you can reach Taran Maran in one day or if you are in a hurry go back via Bahunpati on the road to the Chinese border. Alternatively you can enjoy good scenery by returning via the picturesque village of Patibhanjyang (2200 metres). Follow the Taran Maran Khola which flows from the west, then make a steep thousand metre climb to the village. The trail then descends through the village of Mulkharka and passes through beautiful forests with good views of the mountain range before reaching Sundarijal.

LANGTANG TREK

The peak of Langtang can be seen to the north of Kathmandu on a clear day. In the course of the trek, which takes two weeks, you go to a pleasant valley at the foot of the peak where the glacier ends and the base camp is located. On the way to Langtang you get a good view of Ganesh Himal between Betrawati and Dhunche.

The trek starts from Trisuli Bazaar, a short bus ride from Kathmandu, and for the most part follows the Trisuli River and the Langtang Khola. It passes through Tamang and Tibetan villages like Ramche, Dhunche and Langtang, and finally reaches the cheese factory at 3871 metres set up with Swiss and New Zealand aid.

In comparison to other treks this one passes through relatively undeveloped areas despite the proximity to Kathmandu. This is a more backward region than Pokhara where employment abroad has made some difference. Many Tamangs from this area still serve as porters around the Kathmandu Valley.

An interesting addition to the Langtang trek – if you are physically fit and the weather is warm enough – is a visit to the high altitude lake of Gosainkund at 4313 metres. A different route must be taken from Dhunche and on the way back you can visit Helambu and enter the valley at Sundarijal. The big annual pilgrimage to Gosainkund at the August full moon is unfortunately a bad time for trekking – the middle of the monsoon when the leeches will be out in force.

Most of the Trisuli River's water comes from the Bhote Kosi River across the main Himalayan range in Tibet. It may be advisable to bring some food along on this trek as the Nepalese food obtainable can get very monotonous.

Day 1: Trisuli-Betrawati-Manegaon (six hours walking)

Buses run from Trisuli Bazaar (541 metres) which is 72 km from Kathmandu. Trisuli is the administrative headquarters of a small district and has a 21,000 kw hydroelectric power plant which was built with Indian aid and supplies a large part of

Kathmandu's power supply. The climb from Trisuli is quite gradual until you reach Betrawati (641 metres) where a steep climb starts to Manegaon (1196 metres).

Day 2: Manegaon-Ramche-Bokejhundra (five hours walking)
The steep climb continues to Ramche at 1791 metres after which there are no steep ascents or descents as you pass through Grang (1890 metres) and Thade (1989 metres) before reaching Bokejhundra at 1890 metres.

Day 3: Bokejhundra-Dhunche-Syabrubensi (six hours walking)
The trail goes through dense jungle from Bokejhundra before reaching Dhunche (1966 metres) which is the headquarters of the district. The route then descends to Syabrubensi at 1463 metres.

Day 4: Syabrubensi-Sharpu (six hours walking)
The six-hour walk from Syabrubensi brings you to the village of Sharpu (2590 metres) which is the first village in the Langtang valley.

Day 5: Sharpu-Ghoratable (Langtang) (five hours walking)
Many people prefer not to stay in the village of Langtang but continue to Ghoratable where there is a lodge and you might even find steak and french fries! The climb from Sharpu to Ghoratable is very steep and difficult.

The Langtang trek offers the greatest diversity with the least effort of any trek in Nepal. From 700 metres at Trisuli Bazaar to 3000 metres at Kanchen Gompa, the trail climbs steadily through ever-changing climates and cultural areas. For those who wish to see as much variety of Nepalese countryside and people as possible in a short time, this trek is a must.
Ted Lowe, USA

POKHARA TREKS
The area around Pokhara offers the best opportunities for independent trekking in Nepal, primarily because finding food and a place for an overnight stay is comparatively easy. The Thakali people from the Thak Khola area of the Mustang District have set up many bhattis along the trails. Provided you take you meals there you can usually stay in them for free. These places are quite clean and the food is well prepared although slightly expensive by Nepali standards. In some villages along the trail you can even get pies and bottled beer – due to the influx of tourists in the area. Thakali women are quite liberated and you will find inns run by women whose brothers or husbands have gone to different towns in the course of business.

There are treks lasting from three to 15 days from Pokhara. Some of the most popular include:

Pokhara-Ghandruk This eight-day trek takes you to the beautiful Gurung village of Ghandruk and affords spectacular views of the Annapurnas and Machhapuchhare. A guide is required if you continue on through the forest to Ghodepani; the view from the top of Pun Hill is one of the most fantastic in Nepal. It is possible to reach Ghandruk via Chandrakot on the Jomosom trek and return via Landruk, Dhampus and Hengja. Ghandruk is at an altitude of 2000 metres and is spread out over the whole ridge. It is one of the most famous Gurung villages in Nepal. Many Gurkha soldiers are employed in the British and Indian armies from this village.

Himalayan Lodge, in the upper part of the village, is run by an ex-British Army Gurkha soldier and it's a good place to stay.

Pokhara-Annapurna Sanctuary This 12-day trek continues from Ghandruk to the Annapurna base camp.

Pokhara-Ghachok Lasting only three days this trek reaches 2800 metres and offers beautiful scenery and interesting Gurung villages to those with limited time.

Pokhara-Jomosom-Muktinath This 15-day trek is the best known in the area and some shorter treks form part of it. It's the 'best' trek in Nepal for many reasons. The trekker passes from the paddy fields and forests of the southern hill region right through to the arid desert-like landscape of the Tibetan plateau. The trek crosses right over the Himalayas, although it remains well within Nepalese territory. Between Dhaulagiri at 8137 metres and Annapurna at 8090 metres the Kali Gandaki River carves the deepest gorge in the world; it's crossed at an altitude of 2800 metres. You will see a wide variety of ethnic groups in the many villages you pass through. The trail is surprisingly good, despite the rugged terrain, as it was once a main trade artery linking central Nepal with Tibet.

The first four days of the trek, which goes from 819 metres to 2713 metres, is the same for some of the other Pokhara area treks. From Pokhara you head directly north, crossing a pass at 2835 metres then descend to the hot springs at Tatopani (1190 metres). You then follow the course of the Kali Gandaki River, gradually ascending to Jomosom at 2713 metres. Alternatively you can travel south to Naudanda on the road to the Indian border and follow the course of the Andhi River, cross the minor pass at Karkineta (1600 metres) and pass through Kusma and Baglung before following the Kali Gandaki. Although most trekkers take the first route up and back it is better to go via Karkineta and Kusma and return on the other route as the climb is far more gradual. The fare for flying from Kathmandu to Jomosom is US$58 and Pokhara-Jomosom is US$35. It costs slightly more to fly on a charter.

Day 1: Pokhara-Naudanda (four hours walking)
To make and early start either spend the night in Pokhara Bazaar or take a taxi from the lake area. There are two routes out of Pokhara as far as Naudanda (not the same Naudanda as the one on the road to India). The first route goes up the ridge from the temple of Bindebasini and follows the ridge, known as Kaski, to Naudanda at 1458 metres. This route offers beautiful views of the mountains, Pokhara and the lake. Just before reaching Naudanda you can see the ruins of the palace of the king of the small principality of Kaski. Nepal was once divided into many such small principalities. The alternative route is to walk to the Tibetan refugee centre at Hengja in the north-western part of the Pokhara Valley and then make the stiff climb to Naudanda.

Day 2: Naudanda-Birethanti (six hours walking)
The trail on to Lumle passes through Brahmin and Chetri villages. Lumle has a British-aided agricultural extension project for retired Gurkha service-men from the British army. Three hours walk from Lumle takes you down to Birethanti (1037 metres) on the banks of the Modi River. There are some nice lodges here which make it a good place for an overnight stop and the river has beautiful waterfalls and good swimming in the summer. The route to the Gurung village of Ghandruk starts at Chandrakot.

If you go to Pokhara take the time to visit Birethanti which is only about two day's walk from Pokhara. It is the most beautiful village I saw while in Nepal. The people are very friendly and a series of four waterfalls provides excellent swimming.

Eslie Gill, USA

Birethanti is the closest approximation of heaven on earth – at least for the tourists who can eat bananas while relaxing by the waterfalls!

Steven Smith, USA

Day 3: Birethanti-Ghodepani (nine hours walking)
A straight walk to Tirkhe (1440 metres) takes four hours, followed by a steep climb of 1500 metres to Ghodepani (2835 metres) passing the Magar village of Ulieri and a dense forest on the way. This is one of the highest points on the trail to Jomosom. If you diverge to Ghandruk be sure to take a guide through the forest. This area is bad for leeches during the monsoon. In the spring there are many rhododendrons and in winter there will be snow. An hour away from Ghodepani, which means 'horse and water' in Nepali, is Pun Hill.

On the Pokhara-Jomosom trek, stop at Ghode-pani and the next day climb the hill nearby and you will see about 30 peaks of the Himalayan range.

M Bonnemaison, France

Scene on New Road-Kathmandu.

Day 4:Ghodepani-Tatopani (six hours walking)
A long descent through the pretty Magar village of Sikha (2012 metres) leads to Tatopani at 1190 metres. There is hardly a household in the village which does not have someone who has done military service in the British or Indian armies. The village fives a particularly good view of the Dhaulagiri range and has a ropeway project set up with Japanese assistance. Tatopani has good food and, of course, the hot springs after which the village is named. From here you follow the Kali Gandaki River, one of Nepal's major rivers.

Day 5: Tatopani-Lete (eight hours walking)
Almost all the villages from here on are Thakali and you can expect to be welcomed in all of their homes and offered excellent food. The gradual climb from Tatopani passes through Dana (1448 metres) and Ghasa (2012 metres) to the beautiful village of Lete (2438 metres). Except for a small stretch between Dana and Ghasa the trail is surprisingly good. Lete is in the middle of a deep gorge and offers and incredibly impressive view of the whole of the western flank of Dhaulagiri.

On the Jomosom trek stay in Lete for one night. If it is cloudy have patience, you will see an incredible sunset on Annapurna and the silver Dhaulagiri melting under sunshine.

Gerhard Blias, West Germany

Day 6: Lete-Jomosom (seven hours walking)
The trail continues to follow the Kali Gandaki through many picturesque Thakali villages to Tukuche (2600 metres) the unofficial centre of the whole region of Thak Khola. The relatively affluent Thak-alis have migrated to Pokhara, Bhairawa and Kathmandu since the decline of trade with Tibet. Marfa, further along, has narrow streets and a mediaeval look as well as a government-established horti-culture farm which supplies fruit and

vegetables to the whole region. Jomosom village, the headquarters of the Mustang district, is only two hours further walk. There is a STOL field, police check point and hospital here. This is the last Thakali village as all the villages further north are inhabited by people ethnically Tibetan. The famous temple of Muktinath is only a day's walk from Jomosom.

Jomosom is in an area geographically part of the Tibetan plateau although politically it is still deep inside Nepalese territory. The monsoon never reaches this side of the Himalayas and you will rarely see trees or grass. Just north of Jomosom you may find the black fossil remains of marine animals known as 'saligram' in Nepali. They are from the Jurassic period millions of years ago and are worshipped in many Nepali homes.

Walk up to the yak pastures from Marfa – best done in the warm season when the yak herds are taken up to the high grassy slopes. The walk up and down takes a full day and the path is very dry with little or no water available, so it is best to carry a little. The first part is very steep and rocky but the path gets easier higher up, although the altitude (more than 4000 metres)

may make it difficult. The last part involves a walk round a wide grassy bowl on a slope that carries on up to the snow. From this vantage, the Nilgiri Range is clearly visible directly opposite and one can see a long way north towards Mustang and Tibet; Jomosom and the Muktinath Valley can also be seen.

P H England

Day 7: Jomosom-Muktinath (six hours walking)
The famous Hindu temple of Muktinath is situated at an altitude of 4000 metres and is the final destination of the Pokhara-Jomosom trek. The temple, also revered by Buddhists, is situated at the foot of a snow covered ridge near a cluster of four villages inhabited entirely by Tibetan speaking people. There are also eternal flames which are revered by the pilgrims. Trekkers on their way to Manang climb a 500 metre pass after Muktinath and descend to the pleasant valley north of the Annapurna Ranges. But it is much easier to do it from the Manang side. The village of Kagbeni situated on the banks of the Kali has also been enjoyed by almost all visitors.

Rafting

Rafting along Nepal's mountain rivers has become increasingly popular and Nepal has become almost as well known for its whitewater rafting as for its trekking. In fact many of the adventure trips to Nepal now combine a trek with a rafting expedition, and wildlife expedition in Chitwan National Park. It is interesting to note that rafting on a commercial scale was virtually unknown in Nepal until 1978. The rafting trips mainly take place on the Sun Kosi, the Trisuli and the Kali Gandaki Rivers. *Adventure Travel Magazine* rated the Sun Kosi as one of the world's 10 best rivers for rafting.

RAFTING

No special experience is required for a rafting trip although kayaking, which also takes place in Nepal but to a much lesser extent, is a sport for the experts only. As long as you don't mind doing some paddling and have no objections to wet clothes you're a suitable candidate for a whitewater trip. There are more than a dozen rafting operators in Nepal now but they all follow a generally similar pattern. Costs range from around US$20 to US$75 a day. The tours generally last form about three to nine days and there

are usually between seven and 17 people on each trip. Each raft will have an experienced helmsman, to ensure you stay upright through the tricky bits. More expensive trips may include Nepali cooks and paddlers; on the lower priced trips you take turns at fixing the food and do the paddling.

WHEN TO RAFT

The rafting 'season' follows the trekking season very closely. As with trekking the monsoon season is unsuitable. It's cloudy, damp and miserable and the rivers are often too high. In October, with the close of the monsoon, conditions are at their best. The weather is clear, the harvests are on and the rivers are running well with the run-off from the monsoon. Winter can, as for trekking, be a bit chilly but that doesn't stop the rafting enthusiasts. With spring it's warmer once again and melting snow from the high peaks again provides good river conditions.

WHERE TO RAFT

There are three main rafting rivers in Nepal, all quite easily reached from Kathmandu. They provide a variety of rafting experiences to suit every taste and

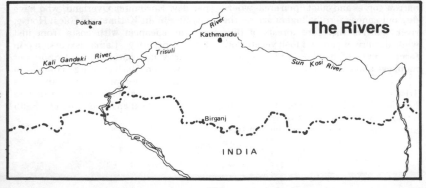

level of expertise. The Sun Kosi, Trisuli
and Kali Gandaki are the three main rivers
used for rafting trips. The first two are the
most popular. Recently, some operators
have started rafting trips on the Marsyangdi River in central Nepal and the
Tamor River in the east.

Sun Kosi River

The Sun Kosi is to the east of Kathmandu
and is the river for those who want a
longer, wilder and more remote adventure.
This is the river rated in the world's top 10
for rafting enthusiasts. The starting point
for Sun Kosi trips is Dolalghat, about 2½
hours out of Kathmandu on the road to the
Chinese border. From there you're out of
touch with 'civilisation' for eight to 10
days for the Sun Kosi runs through a
region devoid of roads or towns. All you'll
find along the way are small villages and
settlements in the occasional open valleys
which the river runs through.

The first couple of days are an easy
paddle but then you have five to seven
days of real whitewater with more smaller
rivers adding their flow to the mighty Sun
Kosi. The final two days are on the Terai
as the river leaves the mountains and you
drift gently down to Chatra where the Sun
Kosi trip finishes. From put-in to put-out
is about 210 km.

The Sun Kosi drains from some of the
highest mountains in the eastern Himalayas including Everest. You raft through
narrow gorges and quiet open areas where
dug out canoes ferry villagers across the
river. Upriver there are forests of pine
while downriver you find lush vegetation,
ferns, groves of bamboo and groups of
monkeys and colourful birds.

Trisuli

Flowing through the centre of Nepal the
Trisuli starts to the west of Kathmandu
and flows south-west to the Chitwan

National Park in the Terai. If the Sun Kosi
is Nepal's river for the more experienced
rafter then this is the river for beginners or
at least those with less experience. A road
follows the river for much of its length.
Trisuli trips generally last from three to
seven days. The most popular trips are a
short 2½-day introduction to rafting – first
an easy day's paddling, then a day of
whitewater and then an easy morning's
drift down into the Terai. Longer trips will
usually include more whitewater rafting in
the narrow gorges further upriver.

Trisuli trips start from the Kathmandu-
Pokhara road. The river flows through
Magar and Gurung areas and in places
you'll see high footbridges crossing the
river. As you reach the Terai the Trisuli
merges with the Kali Gandaki and becomes
the Narayani, a wider, easier river. Trisuli
trips end at Narayanghat from where
many visitors continue to the Chitwan
National Park.

OPERATORS

There are many US or European based
rafting operators with trips costing from
US$30 to $75 per day. You can also
organise rafting trips with *Nepal River
Treks* in Kamal Pokhari (tel 2-15887) for
between US$45 to 55 per person per day.
The can also combine this with fishing.
Great Himalayan Rivers in Jamal (tel 2-
16144) is slightly cheaper and organizes
rafting trips for around US$30 per person
per day. Encounter Overland, who have
an office in the Kathmandu Guest House,
are the cheapest with costs from just
US$20 per day. Lama Excursions in
Durbar Marg charge about US$50 per
day. Also on Durbar Marg, Himalayan
River Exploration probably organise the
best of the Nepal based trips but they're
also the most expensive at around US$65
a day.

Booklist

An amazing number of books have been written about exploring Nepal, mountaineering in Nepal and on its culture, art, religions and architecture. The list that follows is simply a selection of some of the more interesting books. Some of them may only be readily available in Nepal, others are long out of print and may only be found in libraries.

GENERAL

The Wildest Dreams of Kew Jeremy Bernstein, Simon and Schuster, New York, 1970 – a very readable account of Nepal's history and an evocative description of the trek to the Everest base camp.

Nepal – The Kingdom in the Himalayas Toni Hagen, Kummerley and Frey, Berne, 1980 – the definitive record of the geology and people of Nepal by the same man who, until the early sixties, had probably seen more of the country than anyone else – Westerner or Nepali. Numerous personal insights make it particularly interesting and it has the added bonus of excellent colour photography.

Mustang – a Lost Tibetan Kingdom Michel Peissel, Collins and Harvill Press, 1968 – a somewhat over-excited description of a visit to the isolated region of Mustang north of the Annapurnas and close to the Tibetan border/

Nepal Namaste Robert Rieffel, Sahayogi Prakashan, Kathmandu, 1978 – a good general guidebook to Nepal.

Kathmandu Colin Simpson, Angus and Robertson, Sydney, 1967 – an attractive book about a visit to Kathmandu and Pokhara, with some fine photographs.

The Mountain is Young Han Suyin, Jonathan Cape, London, 1971 – a flowery women's magazine-style, fictional romance set in Nepal in the mid-fifties.

CULTURE, PEOPLES, FESTIVALS

Festivals of Nepal Mary Anderson, George, Allen and Unwin, London, 1971 – covers the many festivals celebrated in Nepal.

People of Nepal Dor Bahadur Bista, Ratna Pustak Bhandar, Kathmandu – deals in detail with the different ethnic groups of Nepal.

Rherpas of Nepal C Von Furer-Haimendorf, John Murray, London 1964 – a rather dry study of the Sherpas of the Everest region.

Tigers for Breakfast Michel Peissel, Hodder and Stoughton, London, 1966 – a biography of the well known Boris Lissanevith of the Royal Hotel and Yak and Yeti Restaurant.

The Gods of Nepal Mary Rubel, Shivaratna Harsharatna, Kathmandu, 1968 – a detailed description of the Hindu and Buddhist deities.

A Nepalese Discovers his Country Prakash A Raj, Sajha Prakashan, Kathmandu, describes the social, economic, and political transformation of Nepal since 1951 when it ended its isolation.

Nepal in Crisis Blaikie, Cameron and Seddon, Oxford University Press, 1978, London – describes the reason for lack of development in Nepal in the decades of the sixties and seventies in the context of the construction of roads.

The Heart of the Jungle K K Gurung, Andre Deutsch, London, 1983, describes in detail different kinds of wildlife found in Chitwan National Park.

ART AND ARCHITECTURE

Kathmandu Valley Towns Fran Hosken, Weatherhill, New York, 1974 – more than 500 colour and black and white photographs of the towns, temples and people of the valley and an introduction to its history and festivals.

Nepal - Art Treasures from the Himalayas Waldschmidt, Oxford & IBH, London, 1969 – good description of many works of art in Nepal including photographs of objects.

Himalayan Art Madanjeet Sing, Macmillan, London, 1968 – an introduction to the art of the whole Himalayan region with beautiful pictures.

An Introduction to the Hanuman Dhoka Institute of Nepal and Asian Studies, Kirtipur, 1975 – an excellent description of the old Royal Palace and the many buildings clustered in Kathmandu's Durbar Square.

TREKKING

Trekking in the Nepal Himalaya Stan Armington, Lonely Planet, Melbourne 1985 – everything you need to know before setting out for a trek in Nepal, plus day by day coverage of all the main trekking routes with excellent maps.

Trekking in the Himalayas T Iozowa, Yama Kei, Tokyo, 1980 – translated from Japanese, the book contains good maps and descriptions of trekking trails.

A Guide to Trekking in Nepal Stephen Bezruchka, Sahayogi Press, Kathmandu & The Mountaineers, Seattle, 1981 – a detailed description of the main trekking routes for the independent trekker.

Sherpa, Himalaya, Nepal Mario Fantin – good photographs and a detailed description of the Everest trek and the Sherpas of that region.

Trekking in Mt Everest and Solu Khumbu, Trekking North of Pokhara and Helambu, Langtang Valley and Ganja la John L Hayes, Peter Purna Books, Kathmandu, 1976 – This series of trekking guides gives a detailed description of each of the above treks and even an altitude profile.

A Winter in Nepal John Morris, Rupert Hart-Davis, London, 1964 – a very readable account of a Kathmandu to Pokhara trek by a retired British army Gurkha officer whose fluent Nepali allowed him to make some interesting observations of Nepalese life.

Nepal Himalaya H W Tillman, Cambridge University Press, London, 1952 – if you can find this book in libraries, it gives a fascinating account of some easy going rambles around Nepal by an Everest pioneer of the thirties together with some astonishingly unplanned (by today's standards) mountain assaults.

MOUNTAINS & MOUNTAINEERING

Annapurna South Face Chris Bonnington, Cassell, London, 1971 – an interesting account of the new highly technical assaults on difficult mountain faces plus the problems of expedition organisation and the sheer logistics of carrying out the climb.

Everest the Hard Way Chris Bonnington, Hodder and Stoughton, London, 1976 (also available in paperback) – the exciting story of the perfectly timed and executed rush to the summit in 1975, the first successful ascent by the south-west face. Backed up by some of the most amazing mountaineering photographs ever taken.

Everest South-West Face Chris Bonnington, Hodder and Stoughton, London, 1973 – an account of the author's earlier, and unsuccessful, attempt on the most difficult Everest face.

Many People Come, Looking, Looking Galen Rowell, George, Allen & Unwin, London, 1981 – an interesting study on the impact of mountaineering and trekking on the Himalayan region. Many excellent photographs but a rather steep price.

To the Third Pole G O Dhyrenfurth, Munich, 1960 – the post war attacks on the world's highest peaks, the third pole of the world according to the expedition leader.

Annapurna Maurice Herzog, Jonathan Cape, London, 1952 – a classic description of the first successful conquest of an 8000 metre peak and the harrowing, frostbitten aftermath.

The Conquest of Everest Sir John Hunt, Hodder and Stoughton, London 1953 – first successful climb of the world's highest peak.

Annapurna to Dhaulagiri Dr Harka Gurung, Department of Information, HMG, Kathmandu – describes the mountaineering activity in Nepal between 1950 and 1960 when almost all the major peaks were conquered.

The Himalayas – a Journey to Nepal Takehide Kazami, Kodansha International, 1968 – one of the Japanese 'This Beautiful World' series with stunningly beautiful colour photographs of many of Nepal's peaks.

Himalaya Herbert Tichy, Robert Hale, London, 1970 – a chatty series of incidents and anecdotes from the author's Himalayan wanderings since the thirties, including the ascent of Cho Oyu, at the time the third highest peak climbed.

Faces of Everest – Major Ahluwalliah, Vikas Publication, Delhi 1977, describes mountaineering activity on Everest in detail.

Hashish

One of the reasons for the increasing popularity of Kathmandu in the late sixties and early seventies, particularly amongst the foreign community, was the unlimited availability of hashish and even stronger drugs. Although the smoking of hashish had been free in Nepal until 1973, few local people smoked it apart from the *sadhus* or holy men. Some young Nepalese were starting to smoke as a result of association with foreigners however. Hash smoking is now supposed to be banned but people say it still goes on. Taking hash out of the country is strictly prohibited and several people have been arrested at the airport trying to smuggle it out. A recent study conducted by the government showed that many areas in the hills of western Nepal where people were financially dependent on the cultivation of marijuana had been adversely effected by the ban.

Hard Drugs

The number of hard drug addicts in Nepal is estimated to be between five to eight thousand, mostly teenagers and young people.

In a study done last year, Father Thomas Gafney S.J. of the St Xavier's Social Service Centre made the estimate which medical doctors now believe must have increased considerably.

Hard drug abuse is no more a monopoly of Kathmandu alone but has spread to other smaller townships in the Kingdom, they say.

According to Father Gafney, the list of 'deviant' drugs used in Nepal includes opium, morphine, pethidine, heroin, aminophetamines, barbiturates, and minor tranquilizers like Valium and Librium.

This does not include hashish and ganja (cannabis) which, according to Father Gafney, the average Nepali does not consider 'seriously deviant'.

Opium is used principally by older people in rural societies but is now fast becoming a second choice for urban drug abusers.

According to Father Gafney, pethidine, a man-made synthetic opiate, although locally available only to the medical profession, is also widely used by teenagers and young Nepalis.

But the most 'popular' drug among the young addicts is heroin which is distilled from opium and is about three times more powerful.

from the 'The Rising Nepal', 6.11.84.

Glossary

Apron– colourful aprons are worn by all married Tibetan women.

Ashoka – Indian emperor who did much to spread Buddhism 2500 years ago, including to Nepal.

Asla – river trout.

Avalokitesvara – Hindu/Buddhist god whose incarnation is Machendranath.

Bakba – Tibetan clay mask.

Bajra – see Dorje.

Bazar – market area, a market town is called a bazar.

Bel Tree – young Newari girls are symbolically 'wed' to a bel tree to ensure that the death of any future husband does not leave them a widow.

Bhairab – the fearful manifestation of Shiva.

Bhati – tea shop/rest house in western Nepal.

Bon Po – the animist pre-Buddhist religion of Tibet.

Brahmins – the priestly caste of Hindus who also form one of Nepal's major ethnic groups.

Chakra – disc-like weapon of Vishnu.

Chang – Tibetan rice beer.

Chappati – unleavened Indian bread.

Chautara – stone platforms built around trees along walking trails as resting places for walkers.

Chetris – prince and warrior caste of Hindus, the present king and all the Ranas were chetris.

China Lama – the chief lama at Bodhnath.

Chomolongma – Tibetan name for Mt Everest, 'Mother Goddess of the World'.

Chortens – Tibetan Buddhist stupas.

Chowk – courtyard or market place, as Kumari Chowk (house of the living goddess) or Indrachowk (market area of Kathmandu).

Chuba – long woollen coats worn by Sherpas.

Crow – the messenger of Yama.

Curd – yoghurt, a speciality of Bhaktapur.

Dal – lentil soup that forms part of the Nepali diet.

Deval – Nepali word for temple.

Devangari – Nepali script, identical to Hindi and Sanskrit.

Dhwaja – metal plate ribbon leading up to the roof of a temple as the pathway for the gods.

Dorje – 'thunderbolt' symbol of Buddhist power.

Durbar – palace, the main valley towns each have a Durbar Square, the square in front of the palace.

Durga – terrible manifestation of Parvati, can often be seen killing a demon in the form of a buffalo.

Earthquakes – are rare in Nepal but major ones shook the valley in 1833 and 1934.

Everest – the highest mountain in the world, named after George Everest, the British Surveyor General of India at the time the British discovered it.

Flag – Nepal is the only country in the world which does not have a rectangular flag.

Freaks – the young westerners who wander the east and can be found congregating in Bali, Kabul, Goa and Kathmandu.

Gaines – beggar minstrels.

Ganesh – elephant-headed son of Shiva and Parvati.

Ganja – hashish.

Garuda – man-bird vehicle of Vishnu, often found kneeling before shrines to Vishnu – human-like except for wings.

Ghee – clarified butter.

Ghat – steps down to a river. Bodies are cremated on a 'burning ghat'.

Gompa – Tibetan Buddhist monastery.

Gopis – cowherd girls, Shiva is said to have dallied with them on the river banks at Pashupatinath.

Gurkha – originally derived from the name of the region of Ghorka, it came to be used for all soldiers recruited form Nepal for the British army.

Gurkhali – another name for the Nepali language.

Gurr – a baked, grated potato dish prepared by the Sherpas. **Gurungs** – people from the western hill regions, particularly around Gorkha and Annapurna.

Hanuman – Monkey God.

Hashish – dried resin from the marijuana plant.

Indra – King of the Vedic Gods.

Kali Gandaki – between Annapurna and Dhaulagiri this river cuts the deepest gorge in the world.

Kali – terrifying manifestation of Goddess.

Kartikiya – God of War and son of Shiva.

Kata – Tibetan prayer shawl, traditionally given to a lama when one is brought to his presence.

Khukri – curved, traditional knife of the Nepalese, used with devastating ability by the Gurkhas.

Kinkinimali – temple wind bells.

Krishna – the eighth incarnation of Vishnu, often coloured blue.

Kumari – more peaceful incarnation of Kali. The Nepali name of the living goddess in Kathmandu is also Kumari.

Lama – Tibetan Buddhist priest or holy man, also respectful name.

Laxmi – Goddess of Wealth, consort of Vishnu.

Leeches – unpleasant blood-sucking creatures that appear in great numbers along the trekking trails during the monsoon – to get rid of them use a lighted cigarette, salt or insect spray, but do not try to pull them off.

Lingam – phallically shaped symbol of Shiva's creative powers.

Machendranath – patron God of the Kathmandu Valley.

Mahabharata – ancient Hindu epic.

Mahseer – giant game fish caught in the rivers of the Terai.

Malla – dynasty which ruled the valley from the 13th to the 18th century and created some of the finest art and architecture in the valley.

Mandala – geometrical and astrological representation of the world.

Mandir – Nepalese word for temple.

Manjushree – God who cut the Chobar Gorge and drained the dammed-up waters from the valley.

Mani Stone – stone carved with the Buddhist chant 'Om man padme hum' – oh you jewel in the lotus.

Mani Wall – wall built of these stones in the hill country, always walk by one with the wall on your right.

Mantra – prayer formula or chant.

Mara – Buddhist God of Death, has three eyes and holds the wheel of life.

Mirror – usually found on temples to help devotees place their tikas.

Monsoon – rainy period from mid-June to late-September when there is rainfall virtually every day; there is also a very short winter monsoon, lasting a day or two usually in late January.

Muktinath – holy place north of Pokhara where a natural gas flame and water issue from the same rock.

Naga – serpent deity.

Namaste – Nepalese greeting.

Names – male Sherpas are named after the day of the week they were born; Monday – Dawa, Tuesday – Mingma, Wednesday – Lakpa, Thursday – Phurbu, Friday – Pasang, Saturday – Pemba, Sunday – Nyima.

Nandi – the bull, animal of Shiva.

Narayan – incarnation of Vishnu.

Narsimha (Narsingha) – man-lion incarnation of Vishnu.

Newars – original people of the Kathmandu Valley who were responsible for the architectural style of the valley.

Nilakantha – form of Shiva with blue throat caused by swallowing poison that would have ruined the world.

Oriflammes – prayer flags, prayers written on them are carried off by the breeze.

Pagoda – multi-storied Nepalese temple, this style originated in Nepal and was later taken up in China and Japan.

Panchayat – village democracy, the party-less government of Nepal.

Pashupati – incarnation of Shiva.

Patakas – see dhwajas.

Porters – hill people who carry goods along the trails of roadless Nepal.

Prashad – consecrated food.

Prayer Wheels – cylindrical wheel inscribed with a Buddhist prayer which devotees spin round; in the hill country there are water-driven prayer wheels.

Puja – religious ritual or observance.

Raksi – rice spirit.

Ramayana – Hindu epic telling of the adventures of Prince Rama and his beautiful wife Sita and the demon King Ravana.

Rana – the series of hereditary Prime Ministers who ruled Nepal from 1841 to 1951.

Refugees – thousands of refugees fled to Nepal from Tibet after the Chinese invasion.

Reincarnate Lama – lama who has been selected for his position due to indication that he is the reincarnated form of a previous lama.

Rhododendrons – in Nepal rhododendrons are not a small decorative bush but a huge, brilliant tree which blooms in March and April above 2000 metres.

Ropeway – built from Thankot in the valley to Dharsing in 1929, to bring goods up from India, still in use today.

Sagarmatha – Nepalese name for Mt Everest.

Sankha – conch shell symbol of Vishnu.

Sarangi – violins played by the gaines.

Sherpas – hill people of eastern Nepal who became famous for their exploits with mountaineering expeditions, literally means 'people from the east'.

Sherpanis – female Sherpas.

Shivaratri – birthday of Shiva.

Sirdar – leader/organiser of a group of porters.

Solu Khumbu – Everest region of eastern Nepal where the majority of the Sherpas live.

Sonam – kharma built up during successive incarnations.

STOL – short take-off and landing aircraft.

Stupa – Buddhist religious structure like a circular mound surmounted by a spire, always walk around stupas clockwise.

Shikara – Indian-style temple like Krishna Mandir or Mahabouddha temple in Patan.

Tanka – rectangular Tibetan paintings on cotton, framed with brocade strips.

Tantra – symbolic and metaphysical religious philosophy evolved in the 10th to 15th century that binds Hindu and Buddhist people in Nepal.

Tempos – small three-wheeled transports commonly used in Kathmandu – similar to Thai samlors or Balinese bemos.

Terai – flat land of southern Nepal.

Thakalis – people of western Nepal around Jomosom who specialise in running hotels and bhatis.

Tika – red sandalwood paste spot marked on the forehead as a religious mark and on women as an indication of marriage.

Tribhuvan – grandfather of the present king who ended the period of Rana rule in 1951, the road to the Indian border from Kathmandu and the Kathmandu airport are named after him.

Trisul – trident weapon of Shiva.

Topi – traditional Nepalese cap.

Torana – ornament above temple doors which indicate to which God the temple is dedicated.

Tsampa – barley-flour porridge of the Sherpas.

Valley – until fairly recently the Kathmandu Valley was almost synonymous with Nepal, the country is still a conglomeration of many different peoples and ethnic groups.

Vihar – religious buildings comprising sanctuaries and lodgings for pilgrims.

Vishnu – the preserver, has many incarnations in Nepal.

Yak – main beast of burden and form of cattle in the high country above 3000 metres.

Yama – God of Death.

Yeti – the abominable snowman.

Yoni – female sexual symbol usually found with lingams.

Zhum – female offspring of a yak and a cow.

To watch a sunset, preferably alone near the temple on the river, and see a Nepalese day end is an experience both interesting and educational. You see the water buffaloes washed, the goats being driven home and the sun fade away behind the mountains with Swayambhu in the distance.

Uzi Albright, USA

Index

Traveller's Tales

an illustrated journey through Australia, Asia and Africa

Anthony Jenkins

lonely planet

Cartoonist Anthony Jenkins has spent several years on the road, travelling in 55 countries around the world. Along the way he has filled numerous sketchbooks with his drawings of the people he met.

This is a book of people, not places. A tattooed Iban tribesman in Sarawak, a mango seller in Cameroon, fellow travellers in Nepal . . . all are drawn with perception and (in most cases) affection.

Equally perceptive are Jenkins' written comments and descriptions of incidents during his travels. The combined result is like a series of personal illustrated letters.

This is a traveller's travel book. If you have ever endured an Indian train, watched the world go by in Kathmandu's Durbar Square or tried to post a letter in southern Africa, then opening these pages will be like meeting old friends and will probably give you itchy feet to be on the road once more.

Lonely Planet travel guides
Africa on a Shoestring
Australia – a travel survival kit
Alaska – a travel survival kit
Bali & Lombok – a travel survival kit
Burma – a travel survival kit
Bushwalking in Papua New Guinea
Canada – a travel survival kit
China – a travel survival kit
Hong Kong, Macau & Canton
India – a travel survival kit
Japan – a travel survival kit
Kashmir, Ladakh & Zanskar
Kathmandu & the Kingdom of Nepal
Korea & Taiwan – a travel survival kit
Malaysia, Singapore & Brunei – a travel survival kit
Mexico – a travel survival kit
New Zealand – a travel survival kit
North-East Asia on a Shoestring
Pakistan – a travel survival kit
Papua New Guinea – a travel survival kit
The Philippines – a travel survival kit
South America on a Shoestring
South-East Asia on a Shoestring
Sri Lanka – a travel survival kit
Thailand – a travel survival kit
Tramping in New Zealand
Travellers Tales
Trekking in the Nepal Himalaya
USA West
West Asia on a Shoestring

Lonely Planet phrasebooks
Indonesia Phrasebook
China Phrasebook
Nepal Phrasebook
Thailand Phrasebook

Lonely Planet travel guides are available around the world. If you can't find them, ask your bookshop to order them from one of the distributors listed below. For countries not listed or if you would like a free copy of our latest booklist write to Lonely Planet in Australia.

Australia
Lonely Planet Publications, PO Box 88, South Yarra, Victoria 3141.
Canada see USA
Denmark
Scanvik Books aps, Store Kongensgade 59 A, DK-1264 Copenhagen K.
Hong Kong
The Book Society, GPO Box 7804.
India & Nepal
UBS Distributors, 5 Ansari Rd, New Delhi.
Israel
Geographical Tours Ltd, 8 Tverya St, Tel Aviv 63144.
Japan
Intercontinental Marketing Corp, IPO Box 5056, Tokyo 100-31.
Malaysia
MPH Distributors, 13 Jalan 13/6, Petaling Jaya, Selangor.
Netherlands
Nilsson & Lamm bv, Postbus 195, Pampuslaan 212, 1380 AD Weesp.
New Zealand
Roulston Greene Publishing Associates Ltd, Box 33850, Takapuna, Auckland 9.
Pakistan
London Book House, 281/C Tariq Rd, PECHS Karachi 29, Pakistan
Papua New Guinea see Australia
Singapore
MPH Distributors, 3rd Storey, 601 Sims Drive #03-21, Singapore 1438
Spain
Altair, Riera Alta 8, Barcelona, 08001.
Sweden
Esselte Kartcentrum AB, Vasagatan 16, S-111 20 Stockholm.
Thailand
Chalermnit, 108 Sukhumvit 53, Bangkok, 10110.
UK
Roger Lascelles, 47 York Rd, Brentford, Middlesex, TW8 0QP.
USA
Lonely Planet Publications, PO Box 2001A, Berkeley, CA 94702.
West Germany
Buchvertrieb Gerda Schettler, Postfach 64, D3415 Hattorf a H.